■ SCHOLASTI

MAYAS · AZTECS · INCAS

Wendy Conklin

NEW YORK · TORONTO · LONDON · AUCKLAND · SYDNEY
MEXICO CITY · NEW DELHI · HONG KONG · BUENOS AIRES

Teaching *Resources*

DEDICATION

*I dedicate this book to my father, Calvin Lee Hill,
who continually told me, "Keep your head up!
You're gonna make it." I can only hope that I am
half the parent to my two girls that he was to me.*

Acknowledgements

I would like to especially thank two professors at the University of Illinois at Chicago
for their help on this project. Dr. Joel Palka and Dr. Sloan Williams were wonderful sources
of information regarding the fascinating Mayan and Incan civilizations.

Edited by Wendy Vierow

Cover design by Jason Robinson
Cover photo by Steve Elmore/Getty Images
Interior design by Sydney Wright
Interior illustration by Renée Daily (pages 25, 28, 29, 40, 64, 72, 73, 75, 76, 78) and Stemmer House artists
Maps by Jim McMahon

ISBN 0-439-53994-3

CONTENTS

Introduction 5

The Mayas

Map and Time Line 7

Government, Rulers, and Conquests 8

Stephens and Catherwood's Amazing Expeditions 9

Using Journal Clues to Track the Expeditions 10

Tracing Explorer Routes on a Map 11

The Hieroglyphic Stairway in Copán 12

Writing Mayan Glyphs 13

The Mayan Syllabic Grid 14

Creating a Stela 18

Daily Life 19

The Corn People 20

The Popul Vuh 21

A First Class Screenplay 22

Ancient Mayan Ball Games 23

Mayan Ball Game Trading Cards 24

The History of Chocolate 26

Contributions and Questions 27

The Mayan Calendar 28

Creating a Mayan Sacred Calendar 29

Mayan Math 31

Mayan Math Symbols 32

Understanding the Mayan Base 20 System 33

Mayan Math Problems 34

The Mysterious Disappearance of the Mayas 35

Advice to a Disappearing Civilization 36

The Aztecs

Map and Time Line 37

Government, Rulers, and Conquests 38

An Aztec Election 39

Creating an Emperor's Headdress 40

An Interview With Montezuma II 41

The Conquest of Cortés 42

Cortés and Montezuma II Identity Cards 43

Daily Life 45

An Aztec Mythological Mystery 46

Who Stole the Bones From the Underworld? 48

Interview Clues 49

An Aztec School Report Card 51

A Letter From School 52

Patolli: An Aztec Game 53

Patolli Game Board 54

Contributions and Questions 55

Architectural Palace Builders, Inc. 56

An Aztec Medical Prescription 57

The Mystery of Montezuma II's Death 58

A Court Case 59

The Incas

Map and Time Line 60

Government, Rulers, and Conquests 61

Help Wanted: Incan Record Keepers 62

Using Quipu Math 63

A Civil War Simulation 64

Sim Inca: A New Computer Game 65

The Conquest of Pizarro 66

Daily Life 67

A One-Act Play 68

Children of the Sun 69

Exclusively Inca: A New Clothing Catalog Company 72

Wrapping Incan Mummies 73

Contributions and Questions 74

Real-Estate Ads at Machu Picchu 75

Incan Astronomers: Tracking the Sun 76

Incan Suspension Bridges 77

Designing a Bridge 78

Bibliography 79

INTRODUCTION

Archaeologists and sociologists are still uncovering the amazing accomplishments of ancient civilizations that made the Americas their home. The Mayas, Aztecs, and Incas were builders of enormous cities and roads, worshippers of many gods, rulers of vast empires, and contributors to science.

THE MAYAS Thousands of years ago, ancestors of the Mayas slowly made their way to the Yucatán Peninsula. The Mayas' Classic Period, which included the Mayas' greatest achievements, spanned from about 250 to 900. During this time, the Mayas' architectural marvels included enormous cities with many temples in the form of pyramids. The Mayas recorded their achievements using a complicated writing system of hieroglyphics. In addition to a writing system, the Mayas used a base 20 mathematical system in which numerals were created from three symbols—a line, a dot, and a shell. Using mathematics and astronomy, the Mayas constructed two types of calendars—a solar calendar and a sacred calendar. Mayan daily life centered on the worship of many gods and goddesses, to whom the Mayas offered a special drink that came from the cacao tree of the plenteous rain forests. Sacred ball games took place on large courts and were witnessed by crowds of spectators. Although no one knows why the Mayas abandoned their cities, some archaeologists suspect that the great Mayan empire of the Classic Period fell because of lack of food and extreme consumption of natural resources. Later, wars between the Mayas along with the Spanish conquest of the Mayas in the 1500s contributed to their decline. Presently, many Mayas still live in Mexico and other parts of Central America, where they continue to keep alive the rituals of their ancestors.

THE AZTECS The Aztecs were a warlike people who established their empire in the Valley of Mexico around 1200. During the next century, they built their capital, Tenochtitlán, on an island in Lake Texcoco. This island had four causeways leading to the city. Some parts of these causeways had retractable bridges to protect Tenochtitlán from warring tribes. The Aztecs had schools to educate boys—and occasionally girls. They played various games for entertainment. The Aztecs practiced extreme forms of religious sacrifice to their gods, sometimes killing hundreds of people in a single ceremony. At the height of the Aztec empire, Montezuma II became emperor in 1502. Shortly after Hernán Cortés invaded the Aztec empire in 1519, the Aztec civilization fell. Aztecs who were not killed by the sword often fell to slavery or European diseases. Today, thousands of descendants of the Aztecs live in Mexico, as well as California and Texas.

THE INCAS The Incan civilization began around 400 when small farming communities settled in the Andes mountains and the valleys of present-day Peru. The Incan empire, which began around 1438, included an emperor who controlled many rulers throughout his realm. This network enabled the emperor to keep a tight rule on his people. The Incas built 2,000 miles of roads. Messengers traveled these roads and transmitted information from village to village by word of mouth. The Incas did not have a written language, but they kept intricate records using knotted colored strings called a quipu. They built homes from stones cut so precisely that even a knife could not penetrate between them. These heavy stones were hauled up mountainsides and placed together to form buildings for small communities. Like the Mayas and the Aztecs, the Incas were conquered by the Spanish in the 1500s. Today, many Incas still live in the Andes Mountains, speaking the language of their ancestors and continuing the traditions of the past.

HOW TO USE THIS BOOK

This book was written to give teachers a variety of activities to help students learn about the Mayan, Aztec, and Incan civilizations. Many of the hands-on activities encourage students to imagine what it would be like to live in the past. This resource presents information about government, conquests, daily life, and valuable contributions from these ancient civilizations in an interesting format to make learning exciting and productive. The book is divided into three sections, one for each of the three civilizations. Each section begins with a map and time line, which you may choose to reproduce for students. Each section also includes background information throughout. This information is for your use, although some activities require that you share it with students. It is best to work through the activities consecutively because many of the topics build upon previous topics taught in the unit. As you introduce each civilization to students, begin by using the map and references that accompany each new section. This will help students to understand the time frame and location of each civilization.

A WARNING ABOUT WEB SITES

To accompany Internet-savvy classrooms, various Web sites that can be used to find additional information are sprinkled throughout the book. Before allowing students to investigate these Web sites, be sure to check out each one yourself to determine if it is appropriate for them.

THE MAYAS

Map and Time Line

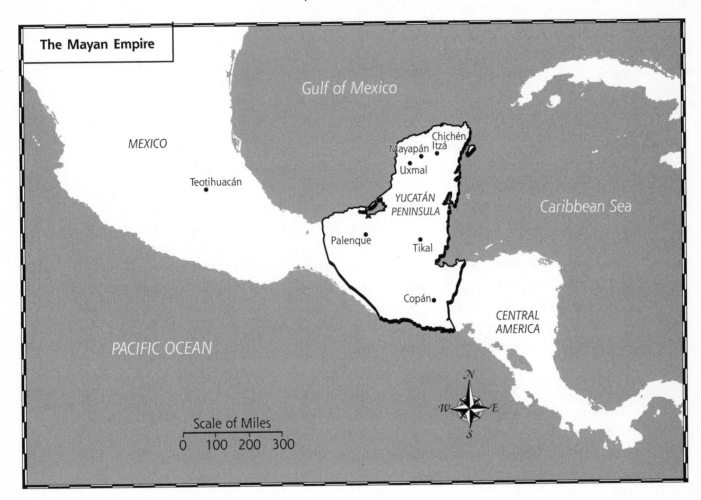

The Mayan Empire

Gulf of Mexico

MEXICO

Teotihuacán

Chichén Itzá

Mayapán

Uxmal

YUCATÁN PENINSULA

Caribbean Sea

Palenque

Tikal

Copán

CENTRAL AMERICA

PACIFIC OCEAN

Scale of Miles

0   100   200   300

N W E S

3114 BC
This date marks the beginning of the Mayan calendar and is the Mayas' creation date.

600 BC
The Mayas begin to build large pyramids.

800
The Mayas begin to abandon their cities.

1200
Mayapán replaces Chichén Itzá as the chief Mayan city.

1527
The Spanish begin their conquest of the Mayas.

1000 BC
Preclassic Period begins. Mayan farmers settle in what is now northern Guatemala.

250
Classic Period begins. The Mayas build great cities and excel in architecture, art, science, and writing.

900
Postclassic Period begins. Chichén Itzá becomes the most important Mayan city.

1440
Wars rage between Mayan leaders.

Today
Many Mayas continue to practice their customs.

GOVERNMENT, RULERS, AND CONQUESTS

Rediscovery of Mayan Civilization

John Lloyd Stephens, an American lawyer and author, and Frederick Catherwood, an English artist, brought the Mayan world to the attention of the public. They set out for the Yucatán Peninsula on an expedition in 1839 to search for the lost city of Copán (koh-PAHN). They found it buried under the rain forest and uncovered massive pyramids, stairways, platforms, and buildings. This find proved true the rumors of this lost city and was the first step in uncovering an entire ancient civilization.

When Stephens and Catherwood reached the ancient cities, each had a job to do. Stephens wrote about what he saw, while Catherwood drew intricate pictures of the sights. After exploring Copán, the two made the long journey to the ancient cities of Palenque (pah-LEHNK-ay) and Uxmal (oosh-MAHL). Their expedition was cut short when Catherwood became ill with malaria, forcing the two to return to New York. After their second expedition to Central America, Stephens published his second book but hardly recognized Catherwood's contribution. Stephens and Catherwood remained friends but never traveled together again. Stephens is called the father of Mayan archaeology because his books opened the way for archaeologists and scholars to examine Mayan culture.

Government and Religion

The ancestors of the Mayas date back to about 1000 BC. These ancestors occupied both the lowlands, consisting of hot, humid jungles, and the highlands, composed of rugged mountains, volcanoes, and canyons. By 800 BC Mayan villages were well established in the lowlands. The growth of cities brought many changes in Mayan government. Kings with absolute authority overtook leaders in small farming communities. These kings were looked upon as semidivine, and it was believed that they were granted the ability to communicate directly with gods who ensured the well-being of the people. This belief led to a close relationship between government and religion.

Record Keeping

The Mayan kings were concerned with keeping records of the past. They erected stelae (STEE-lee), large upright stone monuments that commemorated special events of Mayan culture. Many ancient stelae have been uncovered throughout Mayan territory. A stela usually had a carving of a man on one side and hieroglyphics on the other side. The hieroglyphics noted such information as dates; historical events; information about rulers, government, and communities; and religious ceremonies. This information was recorded at least every 20 years. The Mayas also recorded information in books of paper.

STEPHENS AND CATHERWOOD'S AMAZING EXPEDITIONS

Students organize scrambled journal entries to trace the expeditions of two explorers on a map.

Materials

Using Journal Clues to Track the Expeditions (page 10), *Tracing Explorer Routes on a Map* (page 11), two different colored pencils

Here's How

1. Share with students the background information on page 8 about the rediscovery of Mayan civilization. Tell students that they will uncover Stephens and Catherwood's routes to the Mayan ruins by putting the explorers' mixed-up journal entries in order. (For the purposes of this activity, the journal entries are fictional, although based on facts.)

2. Give students copies of *Using Journal Clues to Track the Expeditions* and *Tracing Explorer Routes on a Map.*

3. Ask students to read the directions on *Using Journal Clues to Track the Expeditions.* Direct students to place the mixed-up journal entries in the correct order.

4. Have students label and trace Stephens and Catherwood's expedition routes on *Tracing Explorer Routes on a Map.* Be sure they use a different color for each expedition. Tell students to refer to the events in *Using Journal Clues to Track the Expeditions* as they plot the expeditions.

Answers:

Using Journal Clues to Track the Expeditions (page 10)
The First Expedition: 3, 1, 4, 2, 5
The Second Expedition: 5, 1, 3, 2, 4

Tracing Explorer Routes on a Map (page 11)
Students should trace these routes using different colors.
First Expedition: Belize City, Quiriguá, Copán, Guatemala City, Comitán, Palenque, Uxmal
Second Expedition: Sisal, Uxmal, Kabah, Santa Rosa, Chichén Itzá, Cozumel Island, Comitán, Tulum

USING JOURNAL CLUES TO TRACK THE EXPEDITIONS

Stephens and Catherwood's journal is completely out of order. Under each expedition, put the events in the correct order by numbering them from 1 to 5. The first event is numbered for you.

The First Expedition

_____ After Copán, we decided to search for the ruins of Palenque. We traveled through Guatemala City and Comitán before heading north to Palenque.

1 On our first expedition, we took a boat from New York and arrived in Belize City. From there, we traveled south toward the first ruin, Quiriguá. Just south of Quiriguá, revolutionary soldiers imprisoned us in an abandoned church for a day.

_____ While in Palenque, we stayed in the wonderful ruins, but suffered from suffocating heat and rains as well as snakes, insects, and scorpions. Catherwood suffered from malaria.

_____ After our imprisonment, we explored the second ruin, named Copán. There, we dealt with a man who claimed to own the idols, and we bought Copán's ruins for $50!

_____ We left Palenque, boarded a ship, and traveled up the western peninsula coast to the wonderful city of Uxmal. The effects of malaria made Catherwood delirious, and he collapsed. We decided to head home to New York so that he could recover.

The Second Expedition

_____ We crossed the waterway from Cozumel Island and explored Coba and Tulum. After that, Catherwood became sick again, so we headed back home—never to return together.

_____ We arrived on our second expedition in Sisal. We set out to finish our work in Uxmal, which took six weeks. Then we headed south to a ruin unknown outside of Mexico called Kabah.

_____ We arrived in Santa Rosa, where the only food was iguana. Then we traveled north to the most famous ruins of the Yucatán, Chichén Itzá, where an ancient road led us to great sites.

_____ We spent several weeks at Kabah exploring, taking notes, and drawing pictures. Next, we traveled to Santa Rosa.

_____ From Chichén Itzá, we went north to the coast, boarded a boat, and traveled to Cozumel Island for our next exploration.

Name _____ Date _____

TRACING EXPLORER ROUTES ON A MAP

What routes did Stephens and Catherwood take on their expeditions to the Yucatán Peninsula? Use the clues from *Using Journal Clues to Track the Expeditions* to trace the correct routes on the map. Draw and label each expedition route with a different colored pencil.

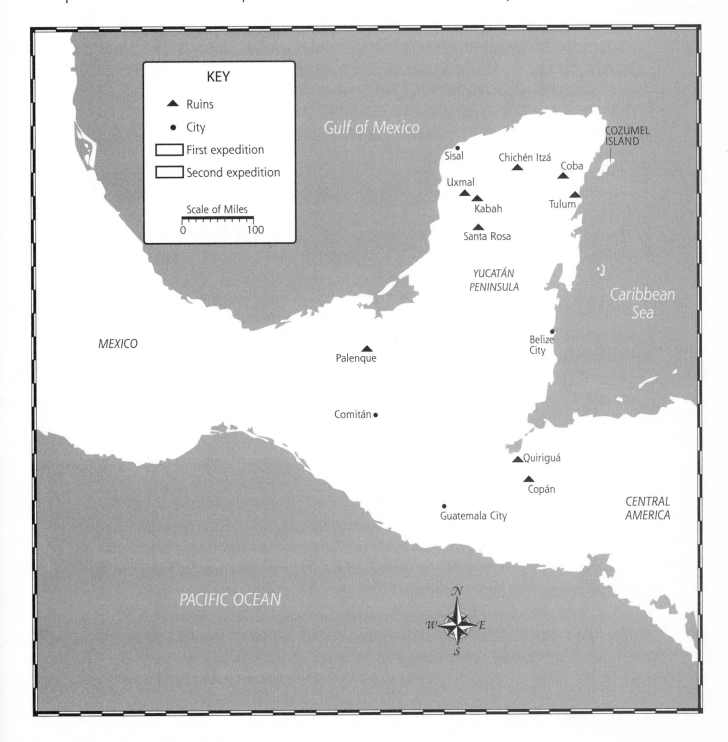

THE HEIROGLYPHIC
STAIRWAY IN COPÁN

Students examine text from an ancient Mayan stairway and write Mayan glyphs.

Materials

Writing Mayan Glyphs (page 13), *The Mayan Syllabic Grid* (pages 14–17), paper, pencils or pens, Internet access or *Reading the Maya Glyphs* by Michael D. Coe and Mark Van Stone (Thames & Hudson, 2005)

Here's How

1 Have students write the letters *A*, *B*, *C*, *D*, and *E* on a piece of paper. Ask students to compare papers with one another. Point out that although everyone has written the same letters, each person's handwriting is different.

2 Tell students that on the steps of an ancient temple in Copán, in what is now Honduras, lies one of the longest single texts from the ancient world. Written in Mayan hieroglyphics, this text lists the history of Copán, including information about the reigns of kings over the span of 400 years. On the stairway, scribes wrote the name of King Yax Pasah (YASH pa-SAH) in a variety of ways for artistic and religious purposes. Point out that just as we have different handwriting, so did the Mayan scribes. Explain that each scribe's glyphs looked different because of his individual style or purpose.

3 Distribute copies of *Writing Mayan Glyphs* and *The Mayan Syllabic Grid* to each student. Explain that a Mayan glyph is a symbol that represents a word or a syllable. Point out that each Mayan syllable represents a sound.

4 Explain that some Mayan words contain many syllables. Point out the diagram on *Writing Mayan Glyphs* that shows how to place Mayan syllables in order. Explain that this diagram shows some ways that syllables of a Mayan word could be written and read.

5 Direct students to look at the first box in a complete syllabary such as the ones found at **http://www.halfmoon.org/syllabary.html** or in *Reading the Maya Glyphs*. Point out that this box shows five ways to write the syllable *A*. Explain that because there is more than one way to write some Mayan syllables, Mayan words can be written in different ways.

6 Next have students read the directions from *Writing Mayan Glyphs*. Have students use *The Mayan Syllabic Grid* to write their names as Mayan words. As a challenge, have students select from a range of glyphs using the complete syllabary you showed as a reference in step 5. Emphasize that some sounds we use are not in the Mayan language. Direct students to substitute Mayan syllables that are similar to sounds found in their names.

WRITING MAYAN GLYPHS

Use *The Mayan Syllabic Grid* and follow the steps below to write your own name. Note that the sounds represented by the letters letters *D, F, G, Q, R,* and *V* are not found in the Mayan language. If your name contains one of these sounds, choose a different glyph that is close to the sound in your name. Use the pronunciation key below to help you choose.

Writing Your Name With Mayan Glyphs

1. On a sheet of paper, write out your name as it sounds in syllables.
   Examples: Savita = *sah vē tah*   Tyro = *tī rō*

2. Find the glyph that best matches each
   syllable in *The Mayan Syllabic Grid*
   (or another syllabary). Remember,
   because the Mayan language does not
   match our own, you may need to
   choose a glyph that sounds similar
   but is not an exact match.

   Examples: Savita = sa yi ta Tyro = te wo
   (There are no exact matches for the syllables
   vē, tī, and rō.)

Savita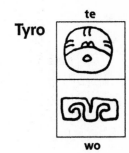

Tyro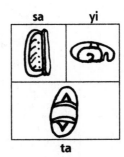

3. Write your name by drawing the glyphs in
   sequence, according to the number of syllables
   and the order shown in the block diagrams
   below. For two and three syllable names,
   choose the block with the spaces in which
   your glyphs fit best.

TIP: If you are using a syllabary grid that shows more than one glyph for a letter/sound, choose the glyph you like best.

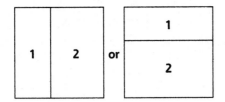

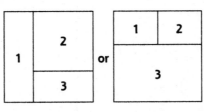

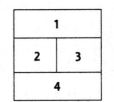

PRONUNCIATION KEY

A as in *bAll*   *U* as in *nOOn*
E as in *grEY*   *X* is pronounced as *SH.*
I as in *bEE*   The symbol ' is
O as in *sO*   pronounced as *H.*

THE MAYAN SYLLABIC GRID

	vowels	b	ch	h
a (aw)				
e (ā)				
i (ē)				
o (ō)				
u (oo)				

Mayas, Aztecs, Incas Scholastic Teaching Resources

THE MAYAN SYLLABIC GRID

	j	k	l	m
a (aw)				
e (ā)				
i (ē)				
o (ō)				
u (oo)				

THE MAYAN SYLLABIC GRID

	n	p	s	t
a (aw)				
e (ā)				
i (ē)				
o (ō)				
u (oo)				

Mayas, Aztecs, Incas Scholastic Teaching Resources

THE MAYAN SYLLABIC GRID

	ts	w	x (sh)	y
a (aw)				
e (ā)				
i (ē)				
o (ō)				
u (oo)				

CREATING A STELA

Students create stelae representing the government of their country.

Materials

Internet access, paper, pencils or pens, modeling clay, pointed yarn hooks or toothpicks

Here's How

© Macduff Everton/CORBIS

1 Show students examples of stelae on the Internet, such as Catherwood's sketch of a Mayan stela at **http://www.mexico-info.com/ mayanstela.htm**. Have students brainstorm ideas about why they think the Mayas erected stelae.

2 Share with students the background information about Mayan record keeping on page 8. Tell students that they will create modern stelae that will include information about their country's government, leaders, celebrations, and important dates. Direct them to include at least two Mayan glyphs on their stelae. (See *Writing Mayan Glyphs*, page 13.)

3 Explain to students that their stelae should be rectangular with flat fronts and backs. The sides (widths) should be plain. Have students sketch the fronts and backs of their stela on paper.

4 Give each student a fist-size amount of clay. Tell students to choose a section of their stelae to carve in the clay. Direct them to carve their stelae sections using a pointed yarn hook or a toothpick.

5 Display stelae sketches and sculptures around the classroom.

DAILY LIFE

The Popul Vuh

Daily life for Mayas centered on their religious beliefs. The Popul Vuh (PAH-puhl VOOH), also known as the Book of Council, tells the ancient record of Mayan religion, traditions, and history. It was passed down orally from generation to generation and reveals the connection between the Mayas' activities and their beliefs. The stories of the Popul Vuh were first written down during the sixteenth century and translated into Spanish during the eighteenth century. The Popul Vuh includes three creation myths—one of which centers on the important Mayan crop of corn.

Ball Games

The Popul Vuh also contains references to ancient Mayan ball courts. Archaeologists and scholars still have many questions about the game that was played on these courts. The games were usually held along with religious ceremonies conducted by the king and priests. These rituals sometimes included human sacrifice, although no one knows if the captives that were sacrificed participated in the games. Mayan ball games were played by two teams in long rectangular courts with slanted walls and stone hoops. Ballplayers probably wore thick padding on their legs and knees to protect themselves, although they were badly bleeding and bruised by the end of the game. The Mayas called this game pok-a-tok, while the Aztecs played a similar game called tlachtli.

Chocolate

One offering that the Mayas gave to their deities during religious ceremonies was a special drink made from the cacao tree, which grew in the rain forests of Central and South America. The Mayas produced chocolate from its seeds. A type of small fly called the midge pollinated the tree. The pollination produced pods, which were cracked open by various animals that ate the pulp and left the bitter seeds on the ground. The Mayas crushed the seeds into powder and added chilies to make a spicy drink. They called this drink chocol haa, which meant hot water. The Mayas also planted the seeds in their own gardens and grew cacao trees in their front yards for convenience. In addition to offering the drink to the gods, Mayan nobles and peasants enjoyed the cacao drink. (The Aztecs also loved chocolate, but only their nobles and upper class drank it because cacao, which was rare in Aztec territory, was extremely valuable and even used as currency.)

THE CORN PEOPLE

Students use corn to construct a representation of a Mayan ancestor.

Materials

corncobs*; glue and tape; items for decorating such as yarn, ribbon, cotton balls, cloth, feathers, buttons, construction paper; index cards; pencils or pens; Internet access; *Tracing Explorer Routes on a Map* (page 11)

Here's How

1 Share with students the information about the Popul Vuh on page 19. Then, tell students the following Mayan creation myth from the Popul Vuh.

> *According to Mayan beliefs, the gods created the earth, sculpting the landscape, planting plants, and creating all kinds of living creatures. Then they decided to make human beings for the sole purpose of hearing praise. First, they tried to make humans out of mud, but it rained and the people melted. Then the gods carved humans out of wood, but the floods came and drowned some of them. The survivors of the flood became monkeys. In a final effort, the gods decided to make humans out of corn. These corn people were the ancestors of the Mayas.*

2 Discuss with students how the Mayas thought of maize as their very flesh and blood. Tell students that they will create a representation of a Mayan ancestor from corn. Give each student a corncob and provide decorating items for them to use.

3 Next, have students use index cards to create identification cards for their corn people. Tell students that their identification cards will include a name and place of residence for their corn people.

4 Have students add a name and a place of residence to their corn person's identity card. Students may wish to search for Mayan names on the Internet at such sites as **http://www.mayadiscovery.com /ing/notes/maya-names.htm** and **http://www.mythome.org /mayanames.html**. To help students choose a place of residence, direct them to pick cities from *Tracing Explorer Routes on a Map*.

Corn people created by students.

* Use real shucked corn, dried corn (available at craft stores), or cardboard tubes (students can draw kernel shapes on the cardboard).

THE POPUL VUH

Students transform a myth from the Popul Vuh into a screenplay.

Materials

A First Class Screenplay (page 22), paper, pencils or pens

Here's How

1. Review with students the information regarding the Popul Vuh on page 19. Tell them that the Popul Vuh includes myths about two males called the Hero Twins. Then pass out copies of *A First Class Screenplay*, and ask students to read the Mayan myth. Before students read, you may wish to explain that obsidian is a naturally occurring glass that was used to make sharp tools.

2. Tell students that they will collaborate with others to write a screenplay based on this myth. Explain that a screenplay is a script that is used in films.

3. Have students form small groups of two or three. Direct groups to follow the instructions in *A First Class Screenplay*.

4. After allowing sufficient time for writing, have groups share their screenplays with the class. Groups can choose to present their screenplays in a variety of ways. Provide students with such options as reading their own screenplays aloud, selecting actors in the class to read the parts, or directing actors in the class to act out the screenplay.

Extensions

If time allows, incorporate persuasive writing into this activity by having students advertise their screenplays as movies for the public. They can create posters that highlight famous (or fictitious) actors who will star in their movies and write catch phrases that will grab readers' interest. Post the ads around the school to generate some excitement. Alternatively, you might have students write reviews of their screenplays and post them on a "movie review" bulletin board for others to read.

Introduce students to other Mayan stories. *The Bird Who Cleans the World and Other Mayan Fables* by Victor Montejo is an excellent children's translation of these stories.

A FIRST CLASS SCREENPLAY

Before a movie can be made from a story, a screenplay must be written. A screenplay is a script that tells the performers what to say and how to act. Some screenplays are based on stories from books. In order to make a story work better as a movie, writers may include conversations and actions in their screenplays that were not in the original story.

The following myth is from the Popul Vuh, an ancient record of Mayan religion and history. After reading the myth, collaborate with one or two other classmates to write a screenplay of the story on a separate sheet of paper.

One day the dark gods decided to invite the Hero Twins to come and play a game with them. Being rude as well as evil, they sent their invitation through a lowly louse. As the louse was on his way to deliver the message, a toad swallowed him. Then a snake swallowed the toad. Finally, a falcon swallowed the snake. When the boys saw the falcon flying overhead, they shot her with a dart. After the falcon fell wounded to the ground, the snake came out of the falcon, and then the toad came out of the snake, and finally the louse came out of the toad. The louse delivered his message and the boys accepted. The dark gods challenged them to a series of tests, and the twins managed to outsmart the dark gods each time. For one of the tests, the twins were put into the House of Utter Darkness, which was a very dreary place. They were given two cigars and a torch. The dark gods told the two brothers that they could use these as lights, but had to return them the next day unused. The two brothers knew that this was impossible. So they placed glowing fireflies on the tips of the cigars and lit their room all night long. On the ball court, the brothers and the dark gods made a bet. Whoever lost would be required to give their opponent a bowl of flowers the next morning. The boys lost the game and were put in the House of Razors, where they battled flying obsidian blades all night long. Finally, they made a deal with the obsidian blades to take them back to the real world. The blades, which did not like the underworld, agreed and stopped trying to hurt the brothers. The brothers knew it would be hard to find flowers while they were locked up in the House of Razors. So one of the brothers took a leaf-cutting ant from his bag and told the ant to go into the garden and cut flowers for him. The ant did as he was told, and the flowers were presented to the dark gods the next morning. Once again, the brothers outsmarted the dark gods.

Mayas, Aztecs, Incas Scholastic Teaching Resources

ANCIENT MAYAN BALL GAMES

Students learn rules for an ancient ball game and create player trading cards.

Materials

Internet access, posterboard, pencils or pens, markers, *Mayan Ball Game Trading Cards* (pages 24–25), index cards, *Tracing Explorer Routes on a Map* (page 11), rubber ball, chalk

Here's How

1. Discuss with students the information about ancient Mayan ball games on page 19. Direct students to look at pictures of ancient Mayan ball courts on such Web sites as **http://www.uwec.edu/greider/Indigenous/Meso-America /ballgame/images.htm**.

2. Divide the class into small groups. Ask groups how they think ancient Mayan ball games might have been played on a Mayan ball court using a rubber ball. Have groups brainstorm possible rules for an ancient ball game.

3. Hand out copies of *Mayan Ball Game Trading Cards* to each student. Direct students to read the information about ball games and compare it with the rules that they discussed. (Explain that scholars still don't know many details about how this ancient game was played.) Ask students to compare Mayan ball games with ball games today, such as soccer, football, or volleyball. Record students' responses on a class chart.

4. Have students refer to the information on *Mayan Ball Game Trading Cards* to create ancient ball game trading cards on index cards (let them sketch their ideas on the reproducible page first). On the front, have students draw a picture of a Mayan ballplayer. Direct students to use the information about playing equipment to make sure that their players are properly equipped. On the back, have students list information about their players, including date and place of birth, the name of each player's team, and ball-playing statistics (encourage them to use the ideas for playing rules they generated in steps 2 and 3). Direct students to choose a birthplace from among the cities from the map on *Tracing Explorer Routes on a Map*.

5. Finally, have two teams of students play a similar version of the ball game. Allow students to choose names for their teams. Draw a centerline with chalk in the middle of the room or playground. Direct students to face each other across a line. Then have teams play the game following the rules from *Mayan Ball Game Trading Cards* and using a rubber ball.

MAYAN BALL GAME TRADING CARDS

Make a sports trading card for this high-stakes ancient game. Be sure your card shows a pok-a-tok player in full gear and gives his statistics. Then trade cards with a classmate! Use the information on this page and the sport equipment page to help you design your card.

How to play pok-a-tok: The Mayan ball game of pok-a-tok was played by two teams on a rectangular ball court that had two slightly sloping walls with hooplike stone rings. The goal of the game was to keep the hard rubber ball from touching the ground. Since touching the ball with hands or feet was prohibited, players used their hips and knees to accomplish this goal. The teams faced each other and played on separate sides of a line much like modern volleyball. When the ball touched the ground on one side of the line, the opposing team earned a point. If the ball happened to travel through one of the stone rings, the game was over and the side who scored won.

Sketch your ideas here first. Then, using pencil and markers, create your own trading card on the back and front of an index card.

FRONT

Player's name

BACK

Key Statistics

_____
_____
_____
_____
_____
_____

Player's name _____

Player's team _____

Date of birth _____

Place of birth _____

Tip

When you're adding statistics for your trading card, think of the things pok-a-tok players might have earned points for—hits or returns, errors, saves, hoops, and so on.

Mayas, Aztecs, Incas Scholastic Teaching Resources

MAYAN BALL GAME TRADING CARDS *(Continued)*

SPORT EQUIPMENT

PALMA

The stone palma was worn during the pregame ceremony. It stood up and was attached to the front of the yoke. It represented the player's superior athletic ability.

MANOPLA

A stone manopla, also known as a hand stone, was grasped in the hand and used to hit the hard rubber ball.

HACHA

A hacha was worn on the side of the yoke. It was carved from stone and was usually in the shape of a deer or eagle. It symbolized power.

RUBBER BALL

The rubber ball could weigh up to eight pounds and ranged in various sizes from a softball to a beach ball. Some balls contained human skulls inside of them.

HEADDRESS

The headdress was made of leather, cloth, string, and feathers.

YUGUITO

Yuguitos were used as knee, shin, and wrist protectors.

YOKE

The yoke was worn around the waist during the ceremony before the game. It was U-shaped and made from stone. During the game a cloth was worn in its place to protect the player's hips.

OTHER "GEAR" NOTES:

• Padded leg guards were worn by some players to protect their upper legs from the heavy ball.

• Shoes with rubber soles were worn during the pregame show. The players played barefoot.

THE HISTORY OF CHOCOLATE

Students create a game about Mayan culture and chocolate.

Materials

Internet access; paper; pencils or pens; game materials such as index cards, posterboard, markers, buttons or other objects for game pieces; chocolate (optional)

Here's How

1 Share with students the background information about chocolate on page 19. Have students view Web sites that discuss the history of chocolate, such as <u>Kara Chocolates</u> at **http://www.karachocolates.com/chochist.html**.

2 Explain to students that they will create an original game to teach others the interesting facts about the Mayas and their love for chocolate. Their game creation can be in any format, such as a flash-card game of facts, a board game, or a kinesthetic game. (See tips below to get students started.)

3 Have students design their games on a piece of paper. Remind them to write directions for how to play their games.

4 Provide students with materials to create their games. When they are finished, let students present their games to the class.

Extension

Allow students to play their games with one another. For an extra treat, let students eat chocolate as they play their games. (Make sure that students have parental permission to eat chocolate and that no students have chocolate allergies.)

TIPS

To help your students organize their games, have them first answer these questions:
- What is the goal of your game?
- How will your game teach about the history of chocolate?
- How many players can play?
- What objects will you use in your game (dice, spin wheel, game board, cards)?
- How will players decide who goes first?
- What penalties (skipped turns, lost points) and/or rewards (extra points, chances to trade places with another player) will players encounter during the game?

CONTRIBUTIONS AND QUESTIONS

Calendars

The Mayas used three main types of calendars. One type of calendar, the Long Count, was used for historical purposes and began its date with 3114 BC. Another calendar, the Haab—which was also called the Vague Year—was used for planting crops. This solar calendar of 365 days was divided into 18 months. Because each month had 20 days, there were five remaining days that the Mayas considered unlucky. Another calendar, the Tzolkin (TSOHL-kin), chronicled the sacred year and was primarily used for religious purposes and naming children. This 260-day calendar was divided into 13 cycles of 20 days. Each of the 20 days had its own name and was represented by a unique symbol. The Mayas usually determined the date by combining the Tzolkin and the Haab calendars.

Mathematics

The math of the Mayas was built on a base 20 system. This base 20 system was also used on calendars. Mayan numerals consisted of dots (valued at 1), bars (valued at 5), and a symbol looking like a shell (valued at 0). The Mayas were the first known civilization to use a symbol for zero. Smaller numbers were written horizontally, while larger numbers were written vertically. For each position going up, the column represented a multiplication by 20.

The Fall of the Mayas

The Mayan civilization spanned about two thousand years and saw its pinnacle from 250 to 900 in the southern part of the Yucatán Peninsula. Toward the end of this pinnacle, the Mayas suddenly began to abandon their southern cities, and records on stelae were abruptly discontinued. Archaeologists and scholars don't know exactly what caused the Mayan collapse and look to the fall of other ancient civilizations for explanations. The Mayas used a method of farming called slash and burn. In order to create more fields, the jungle was cut down and burned. Then crops were planted year after year without giving the soil time to rest. This method of farming reduced the quality of crops until finally crops could not grow in the soil. Erosion set in and even buried Mayan houses. Bone evidence from Mayan tombs show spongy areas on skulls, indicating malnutrition. Some archaeologists believe that the lack of food made it easier for outside warring tribes to take over the Mayan people in the south. Many Mayas moved north to other cities like Chichén Itzá. The cities in the northern peninsula continued to flourish for several hundred more years. But even these cities fell to warring tribes and the Spanish invasion in the 1500s. Mayan civilization and society dwindled, and many Mayas integrated into other societies. Today, thousands of people of Mayan descent live in Mexico and Central America.

THE MAYAN CALENDAR

Students create a version of the Mayan sacred calendar.

Materials

Creating a Mayan Sacred Calendar (pages 29–30), scissors

Here's How

1. Share with students the background information about Mayan calendars on page 27. Tell students that they will be creating part of the Mayan calendar. Emphasize that the sacred calendar was part of a larger calendar that included the Mayan's Haab, or civil calendar—which included the Mayan months.

2. Give students copies of *Creating a Mayan Sacred Calendar* and have them cut out the two calendar wheels.

3. Ask students to try to figure out how the calendar works. Allow time for students to experiment with the calendar and share their ideas.

4. Explain that the calendar fits together with the small wheel rotating inside the large wheel. Point out that the large wheel contains the names of the 20 days while the small wheel contains the numbers from 1 to 13. (Students will learn about Mayan numbers and mathematics in the next activity.)

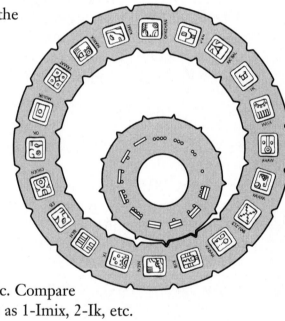

5. Tell students that the Mayan sacred calendar combines the name of a day with the number of the cycle. Point out that we name the days of the week in a similar fashion by combining the name of the day with the number of the month—for example Sunday the 1st, Monday the 2nd, etc. Compare how the Mayan sacred calendar names dates as 1-Imix, 2-Ik, etc.

6. Ask students to line up the day Imix with the number 1. Make sure students have the notches of the two wheels lined up correctly. Direct students to rotate the inner wheel in a counter-clockwise direction until the number 13 is aligned with a day. Ask students to name the 13th day. *(13-Ben)* Then have students rotate the wheel once more and name the next day. *(1-Ix)*

7. Ask students to calculate the number of days in the sacred calendar. *(20 days X 13 cycles = 260 days)* Explain to students that it takes 260 days for the cycle to return to 1-Imix.

CREATING A MAYAN SACRED CALENDAR

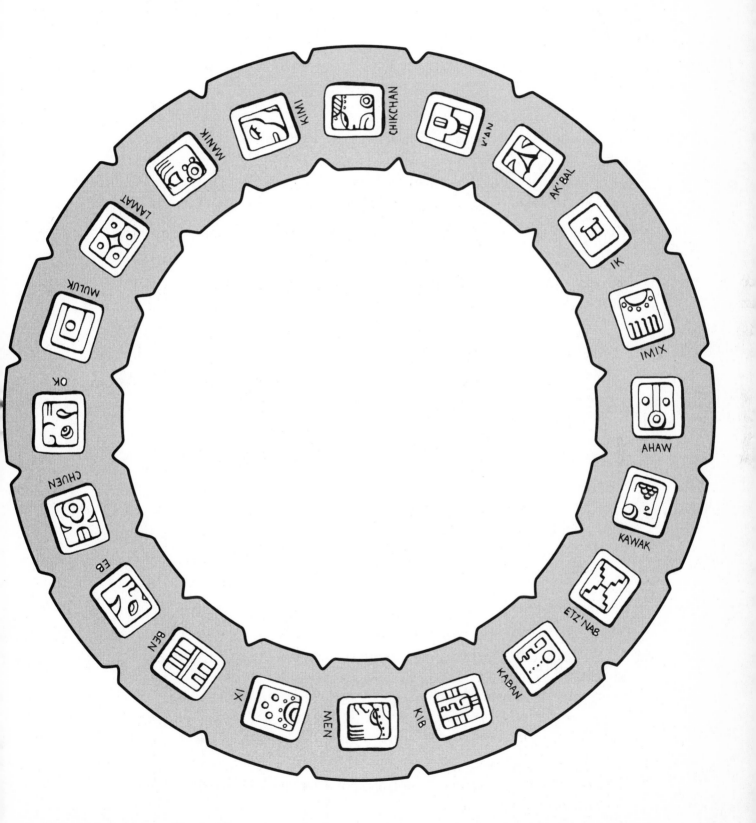

CREATING A MAYAN SACRED CALENDAR (Continued)

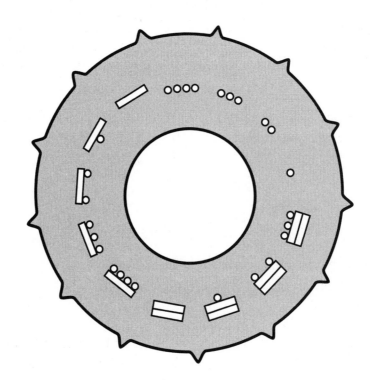

Mayas, Aztecs, Incas Scholastic Teaching Resources

MAYAN MATH

Students use Mayan numerals to solve math problems.

Materials

Creating a Mayan Sacred Calendar (pages 29–30), *Mayan Math Symbols* (page 32), *Understanding the Mayan Base 20 System* (page 33), *Mayan Math Problems* (page 34), pencils

Here's How

1. Refer back to *Creating a Mayan Sacred Calendar*. Have students look at the numerals in the small wheel. Tell students that these are part of the Mayan number system.

2. Ask students to try to figure out how the Mayas' number system works. Allow time for students to examine the 13 numerals on the small wheel and share their ideas with the class.

3. Share with students the information about Mayan mathematics on page 27. Remind students that we use a base 10 system for mathematics. Write the following example on the board to help students visualize how the Mayas' base 20 system differs from our base 10 system. Use the numeral 23 in your example.

<u>Base 10 System</u>

23 = (2 x 10 + 3 or 2 tens and 3 ones)

<u>Base 20 System</u>

● = (1 x 20 or 1 twenty)

●●● = (3 x 1 or 3 ones)

4. Give students copies of *Mayan Math Symbols* and have them examine the Mayan numerals.

5. Distribute copies of *Understanding the Mayan Base 20 System*. Point out that Mayan numbers were written vertically, with the lowest value at the bottom and the highest value at the top. Explain that in the Mayan base 20 system, the value increases by a multiple of 20 when a space is skipped and a new horizontal row is added. For example, the Mayans did not use four bars to write 20. Instead they used a shell (0) in the ones place and one dot in the 20's place. Guide students through the examples and problems as needed.

6. Pass out copies of *Mayan Math Problems*. Ask students to solve the problems on their own. Allow them to use *Mayan Math Symbols* and *Understanding the Mayan Base 20 System* as references. Then have students write their own Mayan math equations. You may wish to allow students to write their equations on the chalkboard for classmates to solve.

Answers:

Understanding the Mayan Base 20 System

1. 16 x 20 = 320   2. 14 x 20 = 280
   12 x 1 = 12   7 x 1 = 7
         332   287

3. 8 x 400 = 3,200   4. 6 x 8,000 = 48,000
   11 x 20 = 220   3 x 400 = 1,200
   7 x 1 = 7   10 x 20 = 200
        3,427   1 x 1 = 1
                                 49,401

Mayan Math Problems

1.
2.
3.
4.
5.

MAYAN MATH SYMBOLS

The Mayas used a shell symbol for 0, a dot for 1, and a bar for 5.

0	1	2	3	4

5	6	7	8	9

10	11	12	13	14

15	16	17	18	19

20	21	22	23	24

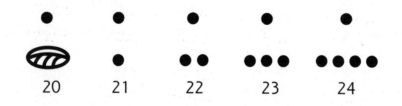

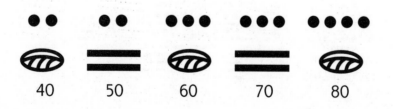

40	50	60	70	80

Mayas, Aztecs, Incas Scholastic Teaching Resources

UNDERSTANDING THE MAYAN BASE 20 SYSTEM

The Mayas used a base 20 system in mathematics. Look at the examples to see how it works.
Then identify the four Mayan numerals at the bottom of the page.

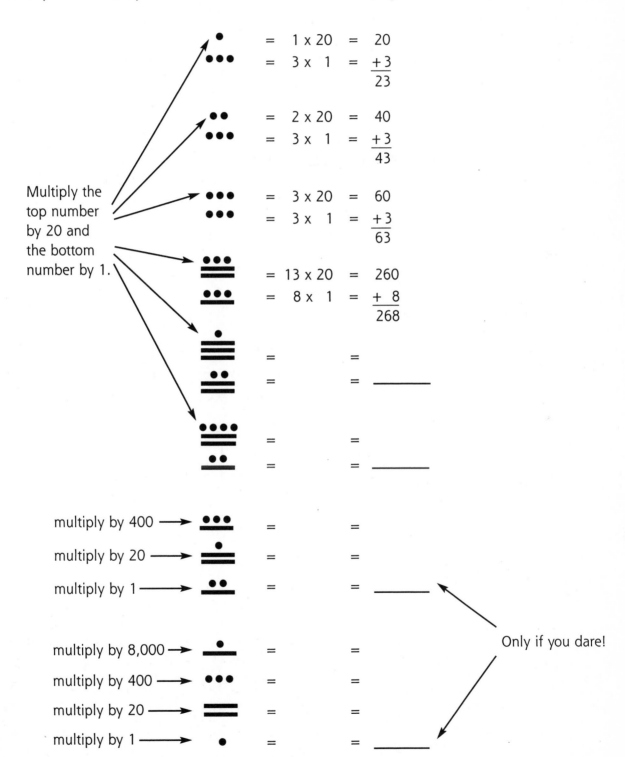

Multiply the top number by 20 and the bottom number by 1.

$\bullet$ = 1 x 20 = 20
$\bullet\bullet\bullet$ = 3 x 1 = +3
23

$\bullet\bullet$ = 2 x 20 = 40
$\bullet\bullet\bullet$ = 3 x 1 = +3
43

$\bullet\bullet\bullet$ = 3 x 20 = 60
$\bullet\bullet\bullet$ = 3 x 1 = +3
63

= 13 x 20 = 260
= 8 x 1 = + 8
268

multiply by 400
multiply by 20
multiply by 1

multiply by 8,000
multiply by 400
multiply by 20
multiply by 1

Only if you dare!

MAYAN MATH PROBLEMS

Solve the math equations below. Write your answers in Mayan numerals. Then create your own Mayan math equation.

1. ≡ + •• = _____

2. •••• + = = _____

3. •⎯ + •• over ═ = _____

4. •••• over ⎯ + ═ = _____

5. •• over ≡ − ⎯ = _____

Write your own Mayan math equation:

Mayas, Aztecs, Incas Scholastic Teaching Resources

THE MYSTERIOUS DISAPPEARANCE OF THE MAYAS

Students offer advice to a disappearing civilization.

Materials

Internet access, paper, pencils or pens, *Advice to a Disappearing Civilization* (page 36)

Here's How

1. Tell students that they will uncover clues to analyze hypotheses about the disappearance of the ancient Mayan civilization. Point out to students that the Mayan civilization saw its height during the Classic Period, which lasted from about 250 to 900 in the southern Yucatán Peninsula. Explain that toward the end of this time, the Mayas began to abandon their southern cities. Tell students that scholars don't know the cause of the disappearance of the Mayas and look to the fall of other ancient civilizations for explanations.

2. List these ideas on the chalkboard: *Invasion, Starvation, Disease.* Explain to students that all three of these theories are viable explanations for the disappearance of the Mayas. Tell students that although scholars have various opinions, most agree that all three were factors.

3. Have students research the disappearance of the Mayas using Web sites such as **http://www.learner.org/exhibits/collapse** and **http://www.jaguar-sun.com/ideas.html**.

4. Ask students to create a cause-and-effect chart on a piece of paper. Have them label causes in one column and effects in another column. Direct students to draw arrows between causes and effects.

5. Distribute to students copies of *Advice to a Disappearing Civilization*. Have students read the letter and write a response on the page.

Answers:

Students' cause-and-effect charts will vary. Possible answers include the following:

Causes	Effects
Slash-and-burn farming ——→	erosion, inability to grow crops, starvation, disease
Warfare ——————→	death, fall of Mayan cities
Drought ——————→	water shortages, inability to grow crops
Overpopulation ————→	malnutrition, starvation, disease

Advice to a Disappearing Civilization
Students' letters will vary, but may suggest alternate farming methods, population control, and peace treaties as solutions.

ADVICE TO A DISAPPEARING CIVILIZATION

In your opinion, how could the ancient Mayas have prevented the fall of their civilization? What advice would you offer the writer in the following advice column? Write a response to the letter.

ASK HELPFUL HANNA

Dear Helpful Hanna,

I live in the ancient society of the Mayas on the Yucatán Peninsula. Our society seems so invincible, but I have heard the statistics concerning the fall of civilizations. Many people say that all good things must come to an end. What advice could you give to my civilization? We want to survive. How do we do it?

Yours truly,

A Mysterious Maya

_____

_____

_____

_____

_____

_____

_____

_____

_____

_____

_____

_____

_____

_____

Mayas, Aztecs, Incas Scholastic Teaching Resources

THE AZTECS

Map and Time Line

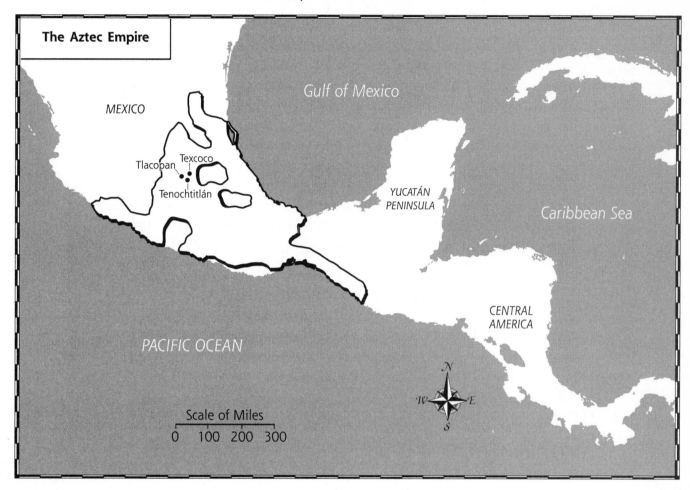

The Aztec Empire

MEXICO

Gulf of Mexico

Texcoco

Tlacopan

Tenochtitlán

YUCATÁN PENINSULA

Caribbean Sea

CENTRAL AMERICA

PACIFIC OCEAN

Scale of Miles

0   100   200   300

N
W   E
S

1200
The Aztecs enter the Valley of Mexico.

1428
Itzocóatl becomes Aztec emperor. Under his rule, the Aztecs become the main power of Central America.

1502
The Aztec empire is at its height as Montezuma II becomes ruler.

Today
Thousands of descendants of the Aztecs live in Mexico and the United States.

1325
According to legend, the Aztecs build their chief city, Tenochtitlán, on an island in Lake Texcoco.

1440
Montezuma I becomes emperor. During his rule, the Aztec empire expands.

1521
Hernán Cortés and the Spanish army conquer Tenochtitlán and the Aztecs.

37

GOVERNMENT, RULERS, AND CONQUESTS

Government

According to legend, the Aztec capital of Tenochtitlán (tay-nohch-teet-LAHN) was founded in 1325. The city was on an island in the middle of a lake (now dry) where Mexico City now stands. Leading to Tenochtitlán were several causeways with bridges that could be dismantled to protect the city. Aztec city-states included pyramid-style temples, ball courts, palaces, canals, aqueducts, dikes, roads, and schools. At first society was organized into *calpulli*, or groups of people who had common ancestors. Later calpulli were physical city districts or zones. Each calpulli elected its own officials and had its own school, temple, and land. Calpulli leaders elected four nobles to its council—one of whom was selected as the *tlatoani*, or ruler. In Tenochtitlán, the tlatoani was called the huey tlatoani ("great speaker"), or emperor. All other tlatoani were under his supervision. Aztec emperors were thought to be related to the gods, and acted as chief priests and military leaders.

Headdresses of Rulers

The Aztec rulers wore elaborate headdresses. Their clothing served as a status of their importance in Aztec society. Only noblemen or valiant warriors wore clothing adorned in feathers and jewels. The Aztec emperor Montezuma II had an impressive four-foot-tall headdress made of green feathers with gold woven throughout. The feathers came from the prized quetzal, a bird that represented wisdom, peace, freedom, and fertility to the Aztecs. It was reported that Montezuma II's headdress was stripped of its gold helmet and brought to Spain. Some people believe that a headdress in Vienna's Museum of Ethnology is Montezuma II's headdress.

The Spanish Invasion

Montezuma II, who ruled from 1502 to 1520, sought to consolidate previous conquests into city-states. His rule was plagued by bad omens, which were realized when the Spanish explorer Hernán Cortés arrived in 1519. When Montezuma II heard that a white man had landed on the eastern coast, he thought it was the god Quetzalcoatl. Stories told how this god of civilization and learning had left his people but would someday return from the East to reclaim his land. Montezuma II sent gifts to Cortés— hoping to keep Cortés from entering Tenochtitlán. However, the gifts whetted Cortés's appetite for gold. Cortés persuaded disgruntled Aztec city-states to help him overthrow Montezuma II. When Cortés entered the city, Montezuma II welcomed him. Cortés had Montezuma II arrested and demanded a room full of gold. He began to rule through Montezuma II. Aztec nobles were upset at Montezuma II's willingness to go along with the Spanish. The Aztecs rose up against the Spanish, and somehow Montezuma II was killed. Two different emperors succeeded Montezuma II.

AN AZTEC ELECTION

Students prepare an Aztec election campaign slogan and speech.

Materials

paper, pencils or pens

Here's How

1. Share with students the background information about Aztec government on page 38.

2. Write the following words on the chalkboard: *calpulli, tlatoani,* and *huey tlatoani.*

3. Present the following scenario to the class: "You are running for election to become one of the four chief officials of your calpulli's council. To be eligible to run for the 'Council of Four' you must be a high-ranking member of your city-state's ruling family. You must also be a good warrior and diplomat. If elected, you will advise the tlatoani of your city-state on important political and military matters. As a member of the council, you will also have the opportunity to someday be selected as the tlatoani. This privilege carries much responsibility. As your city-state's tlatoani, you must serve the huey tlatoani, or 'great speaker,' who is emperor of the Aztec government and head priest. Why should the Aztec tribal leaders in your calpulli elect you? Prepare a campaign slogan and election speech to present to your calpulli to convince them that you are the right person for the job."

4. Allow students to work individually to create their slogans and campaign speeches. Tell them that their speeches should run about one to two minutes long, introduce them as a candidate, and give at least three reasons why they should be elected to their calpulli. (See the tip box below for ideas to help students with their slogans and speeches.)

5. Have students present their slogans and speeches to the tribal leaders of the calpulli, as represented by their classmates.

6. Have students hold a mock election in response to the campaign speeches.

TIPS

Ask students the following questions to guide a discussion that builds background for this activity:

- What are some popular one-sentence slogans from your favorite fast food restaurants?
- How do those slogans sell the products?
- What are some things that a politician might want to promise the people he or she represents?
- What one-line slogan could sum up your intentions as an Aztec politician?

CREATING AN EMPEROR'S HEADDRESS

Students design and create a new headdress for the Aztec emperor Montezuma II.

Materials

paper; pencils; Internet access; markers or colored pencils; scissors; rulers; posterboard; tape; glue; decorations including feathers, beads, plastic jewels; packing tape; 30-inch segment of thick cotton string per student

Here's How

1. Ask students to explain how they know if someone is important in their society. Ask if clothing has anything to do with someone's status in society.

2. Share with students the background information about the headdresses of Aztec rulers on page 38. Have students compare the dress of an Aztec leader with an American leader by creating a Venn diagram on a piece of paper. (Encourage students to compare symbols used by U.S. presidents, such as the eagle on the presidential seal, with symbols used by Montezuma II, such as the quetzal.)

3. Have students conduct research on the Internet at sites such as **http://www.ethno-museum.ac.at/en/collections/namerica/amexico.html** to view the headdress that some experts believe was worn by the emperor Montezuma II.

4. Tell students that they will participate in a contest to design a new headdress for Montezuma II. Ask students to name their headdress. For example, a headdress with many colors might be called "the Rainbow Headdress." Have students sketch out ideas for a new headdress and write their concepts on the back of their sketches.

5. Have each student cut a 2" x 24" strip from a posterboard and tape it to create a headband. Direct students to glue or tape decorations such as feathers, plastic jewels, and beads to their headbands. Have them use packing tape to secure a piece of 30"-long thick cotton string to the inside of the headband. Make sure that students center the string. They should secure only the middle 12" and allow the excess string to hang down both sides. Students can use the string to tie their headbands to prevent slipping.

6. Allow students to choose different categories for awards, such as most creative concept, most colorful, and most feathered. Have someone acting as Montezuma II come into class once the headdresses are complete and present the awards.

AN INTERVIEW WITH MONTEZUMA II

Students create a television show that features an interview with the Aztec emperor Montezuma II.

Materials

reference sources such as encyclopedias and the Internet, paper, pencils or pens, video equipment (optional)

Here's How

1. Group students in pairs. Tell students that they work for a popular television show that frequently interviews celebrities. Students can choose to work for a news show, late-night comedy show, talk show, self-help program, or other type of show. Explain to students that the next celebrity to appear on their show is Montezuma II, the ruler of the Aztecs.

2. Have students write questions to ask Montezuma II about subjects including his looks, his accomplishments, and the way he ruled his people. (See the tip box below for examples of interview questions students might ask.) Have students research the answers using reference books and the Internet.

3. After students have written their questions and answers for Montezuma II, let pairs role-play the scene with one student as Montezuma II and the other student as the interviewer.

Extension

If video equipment is available, have students videotape their shows. Then let students critique the different shows and the types of questions asked.

TIPS

Have students consider how they might phrase questions for the type of television show they've chosen. For example, here are some program-appropriate interview questions a host might ask:

- news show: How and when did you rise to power as ruler of the Aztecs?
- late-night comedy show: What do the Aztecs like to do in their spare time?
- talk show: Tell us about your famous headdress. How is it made and when do you wear it?
- self-help program: Can you offer insights into why the Aztecs offer sacrifices? How do you think your people feel about this ritual?

THE CONQUEST OF CORTÉS

Students reenact the day that Hernán Cortés met Montezuma II.

Materials

Cortés and Montezuma II Identity Cards (pages 43–44), scissors, paper, pencils or pens, reference books, Internet access (optional)

Here's How

1. Tell students that they will reenact the day when the Spanish explorer Hernán Cortés and rebelling tribes, conquered by the Aztecs, met with the Aztec ruler, Montezuma II. Divide students into groups of three so that each student represents one of these identities: Hernán Cortés, Montezuma II, or a rebelling tribal leader.

2. Give each group a copy of *Cortés and Montezuma II Identity Cards*. Have groups cut apart the cards and read their specific scenarios. Then ask students to write a journal entry on a separate piece of paper about their fears and hopes on that eventful day.

3. Have groups reenact the conflict between Cortés, a rebelling tribal leader, and Montezuma II. Encourage groups to add additional dialogue that reflects their ideas about the actual event. Ask students if their characters can come to an agreement among themselves. If so, allow students to write a peace treaty.

4. After the reenactment, have groups research the encounter of Cortés, rebelling tribal leaders, and Montezuma II. Share with students the information on page 38 about the Spanish invasion. Then have groups compare the actual event with their simulations on a Venn diagram.

Extension

Have groups rework their reenactments to correspond to the new historical information they've learned. They may wish to add additional scenes to include more historical facts. Allow groups to perform their revised versions for the class.

CORTÉS AND MONTEZUMA II IDENTITY CARDS

HERNÁN CORTÉS

In 1519 you sail with guns, more than ten ships, more than 500 men, and fewer than 20 horses from Cuba to the Yucatán Peninsula in search of gold. You claim one of the ports where you land and name it La Villa Rica de la Vera Cruz (today called Veracruz). There, you are selected by the new town council to be the captain general, or chief administrator. You state that you are no longer under the authority of your superior, the Spanish governor of Cuba, and claim allegiance only to the King of Spain—Charles V. You destroy your fleet of ships so that your men will not think of going back and will accept your authority. You then write a letter to King Charles V asking his blessing on your title and mission. You manage to convince him by stressing the importance of converting the native people to Christianity. You also mention the wealth of the Atzecs in your letter.

You set out with your men and translators to find people willing to fight against the Aztecs. This is not hard to do because residents of many Aztec city-states want to overthrow the Aztec government and its leader Montezuma II. These people are angry with the Aztec government for imposing harsh taxes and sacrificing their people on a regular basis. You travel over treacherous terrain to reach the Aztec capital of Tenochtitlán (tay-nohch-teet-LAHN). Several causeways lead to this great city, which is set in the middle of a lake. Montezuma II treats you well. He shows you gold and gives you gifts. You do not expect to be treated so kindly.

CORTÉS AND MONTEZUMA II IDENTITY CARDS (Continued)

MONTEZUMA II AND HIS ALLIES

You hear that strange visitors are traveling around the Yucatán Peninsula. It is reported that mountains were actually floating on the sea! These visitors landed in a year that the god of civilization, Quetzalcoatl, may return from the East. You believe that it is Quetzalcoatl, who had been forced to leave his people but would someday return to reclaim his land. This must be the fulfillment of the ancient prophecy. The next report you receive states that these visitors are made of metal armor and look like half deer, half person.

Another report says that these visitors have weapons that shoot fire. Word has spread that these visitors are intimidating other tribes under your jurisdiction to side with them. You worry that the visitors will reach Tlaxcala. You have been taking their people captive to be used in religious sacrifices. You also know that your empire is mighty and that these visitors number less than 600. Your city is located in the middle of a lake with several causeways leading to it. On some parts of the causeway, you have wooden bridges that can be removed to keep armies from attacking. Do you feel threatened and react with force, or do you try to appease these visitors?

REBELLING TRIBAL RULER UNDER AZTEC RULE

You are a ruler who is hostile to the rule of the Aztecs. Your city-state belongs to the Aztec empire. You want to overthrow the government of the Aztecs because Montezuma II, their leader, has imposed harsh taxes on your people. He also has taken many of your people to sacrifice to their gods. The Spanish soldier Hernán Cortés and his small army approach you and ask for an alliance. If you refuse Cortés, you might die. You have seen the fire that comes from the weapons carried by his soldiers. If you go against Montezuma II and are captured by the Aztecs, you will surely be killed for treason. What will you do?

DAILY LIFE

Religion

The Aztecs believed that the success of their daily life depended on the blessings of their deities. They believed their gods controlled the rising of the sun, military success, personal prosperity, flourishing crops, and other events. The Aztecs worshipped hundreds of gods and goddesses, including more than 40 main deities. These many deities were absorbed from the many cultures in the Aztec empire. The functions of Aztec deities in society sometimes overlapped. For example, there were several gods and goddesses who were associated with the harvest. The Aztecs offered these deities sacrifices, including human sacrifices, to keep them happy. On a daily basis, priests attended to the needs of these deities through rituals at local temples and shrines.

Schooling

The Aztecs trained children as young as 4 years old to take on responsibilities. Children were educated at home for at least the first ten years of their life, with mothers educating their daughters and fathers teaching their sons. After the age of 10, boys could begin to attend two different kinds of schools. A telpochcalli was a local school for commoners that was run by elders in the community. Boys who attended this school studied subjects including warfare, trade skills, history, religion, and proper behavior. A calmecac was a school for children of nobility with attachments to the temples. Girls might also attend temple schools to become priestesses. Calmecac schools were run under severe and strict priests. On rare occasions, commoners were allowed to attend a calmecac if they showed tremendous promise. These students learned subjects including the workings of the calendar, religion, songs, poetry, history, speech, law, military arts, and writing. Boys might also attend a cuicacalli, or a military school, where they were trained in the arts of war.

Games

The Aztecs enjoyed the ancient ball game of tlachtli (TLAWCH-tlee). This game was similar to the Mayan game of pok-a-tok. The Aztecs also enjoyed betting on games. In the game of patolli, the Aztecs might bet possessions such as their homes, crops, and even their families' freedom. The board game of patolli used beans for dice to advance around spaces displayed in a cross-shaped pattern. The game would end when one player lost all of his markers to his opposing competitor.

AN AZTEC MYTHOLOGICAL MYSTERY

Students learn about Aztec religion and DNA fingerprinting while solving a mystery.

Materials

Who Stole the Bones From the Underworld? (page 48), *Interview Clues* (pages 49–50), scissors, file folders, paper, pencils or pens

Here's How

① Make a copy of *Interview Clues*. Cut along the dotted lines to separate the clues. Place each clue in a separate file folder labeled with the corresponding deity's name.

② Share with students the background information about Aztec religion on page 45.

③ Give students copies of *Who Stole the Bones From the Underworld?* Read the directions and scenario aloud to students. Ask students to read the rest of the information on the page. Then ask them to examine the DNA sample of the culprit at the bottom of the page.

④ Give students a brief overview of DNA fingerprinting. Point out that a DNA fingerprint is not literally a fingerprint. Explain that DNA stands for deoxyribonucleic acid and is found in the nucleus of every living cell. Tell students that DNA has all of a person's genetic information: eye color, hair type and color, blood type, fingerprints, what types of diseases a person might be prone to, etc. Explain that to get a DNA fingerprint from a person, a DNA sample is taken from hair, tissue, or a body fluid. Tell students that the sample is mixed with enzymes that separate the DNA into bandlike patterns. Explain that these patterns of black bars make up the DNA fingerprint that can be used by crime labs.

⑤ Allow students to take turns requesting the file folders on each deity. Explain that each folder contains interview notes with an Aztec deity about the crime, as well as a DNA sample of that deity. Direct students to compare these DNA samples to the DNA sample found at the crime scene as shown on *Who Stole the Bones From the Underworld?* to find the correct match.

⑥ When a student believes that he or she has the information necessary to convict a suspect, have him or her write down the name of the suspect. Ask students to keep the information confidential until everyone has a chance to solve the crime.

AN AZTEC MYTHOLOGICAL MYSTERY *(Continued)*

7 After all students have named their suspects, tell the class that Quetzalcoatl is the culprit. His blood matches the DNA sample. Read the following confession to the class. Tell students that this is an Aztec creation story about how humans were created.

"It is true, I did it. I agreed to go down to the underworld and gather the bones in order to make people again. If this plan worked, it would be the fifth time—and hopefully the last time—that humans were created. You see, the gods had tried to create humans on four different occasions only to have them destroyed by different catastrophes—once by a tiger, next by a hurricane, then by a fire, and finally by a flood. I had tried talking with Mictlantecuhtli about allowing me to take the bones, and he agreed if I could follow a simple task. He gave me a broken horn and told me to blow it as I circled the underworld four times. I did what he asked and then took the bones. Mictlantecuhtli was angry at my success and chased me. On my way out, I was in a hurry and a quail startled me. I fell, breaking the bones into different sizes. I must have also dropped the note from Huitzilopochtli. He and the other good gods were in agreement that humans should be made to fill the earth. I quickly mixed the bones with blood and created the human race. Because the bones were broken, the humans came out in different sizes and shapes."

WHO STOLE THE BONES FROM THE UNDERWORLD?

It is your job to find out who stole the bones from the underworld. You must examine interview notes with Aztec deities and use DNA samples, as well as the process of deduction, to conclude who did it.

SCENARIO:

Mictlantecuhtli (meek-tlahn-tay-COO-tlee) awoke late the morning of the crime in his usual place, the underworld. He says that he was tending to his pets—the owls and spiders that accompany him—when he discovered that the bones of the dead, over which he kept watch, were missing. Most of the gods and goddesses have alibis, but their information needs to be confirmed. It's your job to solve the mystery of the missing bones!

WHAT WE KNOW:

✔ The crime occurred this morning at 10:00 in the underworld.

✔ The weather was volatile, with thunder and lightning everywhere.

✔ The bones of the dead were missing.

✔ A chase occurred between the culprit and Mictlantecuhtli.

✔ A note with Huitzilopochtli's signature was found near the scene. It read, "Dear Brother, I'll meet you at the usual place around 10:30. Bring the bones with you."

✔ Blood was found at the scene.

✔ All gods and goddesses agreed to give blood samples to be used as DNA evidence.

LIST OF SUSPECTS:

Coyolxauhqui (ko-yol-SHA-kee)

Huitzilopochtli (huits-il-o-POCH-tlee)

Mictlantecuhtli (meek-tlahn-tay-COO-tlee)

Paynal (pa-NAL)

Quetzalcoatl (ket-sal-ko-AT-al)

Tezcatlipoca (tets-kat-li-PO-ka)

Tlaloc (TLAHL-lock)

Xilonen (shi-LO-nin)

Here is the culprit's DNA fingerprint found at the scene of the crime.

INTERVIEW CLUES

Coyolxauhqui

The moon goddess glows in the dark night to light up the world around her. She has been in a constant feud with her brother, Huitzilopochtli, the sun god, for cutting off her head and throwing it to the sky. She claimed to be sleeping the morning of the crime. No one can verify her alibi.

Huitzilopochtli

On the morning of the incident the sun god and god of war, Huitzilopochtli, asked Paynal to deliver a note to his brother. Huitzilopochtli seemed nervous during questioning. Huitzilopochtli is known for his fighting and shines brightly in the sky for all to see during the day. All the gods and goddesses respect him.

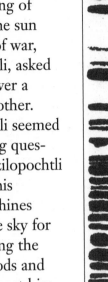

Mictlantecuhtli

Mictlantecuhtli, the god of the dead and the underworld (Mictlan), awoke late on the morning of the crime and hurriedly began working. He claimed that he was busy tending to his pets when he discovered the bones were missing. He heard the culprit, began chasing him, but failed to apprehend him. He did, however, cause the culprit to fall.

Paynal

Paynal, the messenger to Huitzilopochtli, claimed to have delivered a message from Huitzilopochtli to Quetzalcoatl the morning of the crime. Paynal was late getting back to Huitzilopochtli by at least 30 minutes and blamed it on the bad weather.

Quetzalcoatl

Quetzalcoatl, the god of civilization and learning, claimed to be taking care of some unfinished business on the day of the crime. He pleaded the right to remain silent and refused to answer any other questions. His alibi cannot be confirmed by anyone.

Tezcatlipoca

Tezcatlipoca, the husband of Xilonen and the god of night and sorcery, was wearing his jaguar costume on the night before the crime. His costume's spots symbolized the starry night sky. The morning of the crime, he claimed to be staring into his sorcerer's mirror. He said that although he watches others with his mirror, he wasn't spying on the gods that day.

Tlaloc

Tlaloc, the rain god, has been upset and threatening to make thunder with rattles, hurl lightening, unleash hurricanes, and send down rain. On the day of the crime, he created a thunderstorm with lightning. In addition, Tlaloc and Mictlantecuhtli were having trouble getting along. They were arguing the night before the crime.

Xilonen

Xilonen, the wife of Tezcatlipoca and goddess of maize— or what we call corn— was having a poor year. Maize, the most important Aztec crop, was just not growing due to lack of rain. Because of this, she was having problems getting along with Tlaloc. The morning of the crime she claimed to be ironing her husband's jaguar costume.

AN AZTEC SCHOOL REPORT CARD

Students plan a schedule for a day at an Aztec school and create an Aztec report card.

Materials

A Letter From School (page 52), paper, pens, construction paper

Here's How

❶ Share the background information about Aztec schooling on page 45 with students. Copy and distribute *A Letter From School*.

❷ Divide the class into small groups. Direct groups to read the letter and discuss its content.

❸ Have groups compare calmecac and telpochcalli schools. Then ask groups to compare a calmecac school with their own school using a Venn diagram.

❹ Tell students that they have been hired by an Aztec priest to be a tour guide for prospective students at a calmecac. To do a good job, they must plan out a school schedule. Have groups use this letter to help them plan out a school day for prospective calmecac students. Encourage them to make a schedule using a simple, three-column chart with the headings Time, Subject, and Lesson or Activity.

Aztec School Schedule

Time	Subject	Lesson or Activity

❺ Explain to students that it is not known how students were assessed. Ask groups to brainstorm what an Aztec report card might include. Direct them to think about how Aztec report cards would be different from their own. Ask students if they think students might receive grades, comments, rubric scores, rankings, or some other type of assessment report. Have groups create a report card on construction paper for a student at a telpochcalli.

A LETTER FROM SCHOOL

Dear Friend,

I am a son of a nobleman and attend a school called a calmecac. Most of my friends in school are sons of nobles, but there are a few commoners in my class. Most sons of commoners go to a different school called a telpochcalli. Students at a telpochcalli study religion, history, traditions, warfare, arts, and crafts. This school prepares its students for specific trades and crafts.

However, there are a few commoners who are really gifted and are allowed to learn with us at our calmecac. I have the opportunity to study about religion, history, and military leadership. We learn about the festivals and their meanings, how to read calendars, how to address the gods and goddesses properly, and how to perform religious rituals. Novices preparing for the priesthood learn astronomy and how to interpret dreams and omens. Novice priests also help the established priests with sacrifices, offering incense and sweeping the temple area. There are also some girls who are studying at the temple to become priestesses. If any of us are appointed as judges after graduation, we are well prepared because we study law. I think that the most important subject, however, is rhetoric, or speech. This subject is woven throughout all the other subjects. We are able to recite moving speeches for all occasions. By the time we finish school, we will be among the greatest orators in Aztec society.

Our rules are very strict. We are punished severely if we misbehave. This is not much different from our home life as young children. My parents expect me to always obey or else I am tied up and left outside all night with no blankets. Some of my friends disobey their parents and are forced to inhale chili smoke. Needless to say, our discipline in school is strictly enforced.

Well, that is all for now. I must go memorize my lines of poetry for my next speech.

Your friend,
Tecocol

PATOLLI: AN AZTEC GAME

Students play a strategic board game called patolli.

Materials

five kidney beans marked with a dot on one side, six red markers, six blue markers, *Patolli Game Board* (page 54)

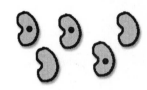

Here's How

1. Two players or two teams can play the game. Each player or team starts with six markers of the same color. The goal is capture your opponent's markers while moving your own markers safely from start to home. Home is the space preceding the square where the player began.

2. Players alternate turns, throwing the beans. To enter the game, players must throw a 1 using all five beans (only one bean may land dot-side up). After throwing a 1, a player places one of his or her markers on one of the four center squares on the board. A player may enter a new marker on any turn, provided the player has rolled a 1.

3. Players advance their markers in a clockwise direction by throwing the beans and moving their markers the total sum of dots shown on the beans. (1 = one space, 2 = two spaces, 3 = three spaces, 4 = four spaces, 5 = five spaces.) For an extra challenge, let students double some numbers (e.g., 3 = six spaces).

4. If a space is already occupied, a player cannot move his or her marker there. However, markers resting on any of the four central squares can be captured by a player who lands exactly on that square.

5. If a player lands on one of the 16 black triangles, that player must give the other player two markers.

6. If a player lands on one of the rounded ends, that player takes another turn. In addition, the player's opponent must give up a marker.

7. The game is over when all of a player's markers are removed from the board. One player will have more markers than the other.

8. If you wish to continue playing, the game begins again with one player richer and the other player poorer. The game is played repeatedly until one player is bankrupt.

PATOLLI GAME BOARD

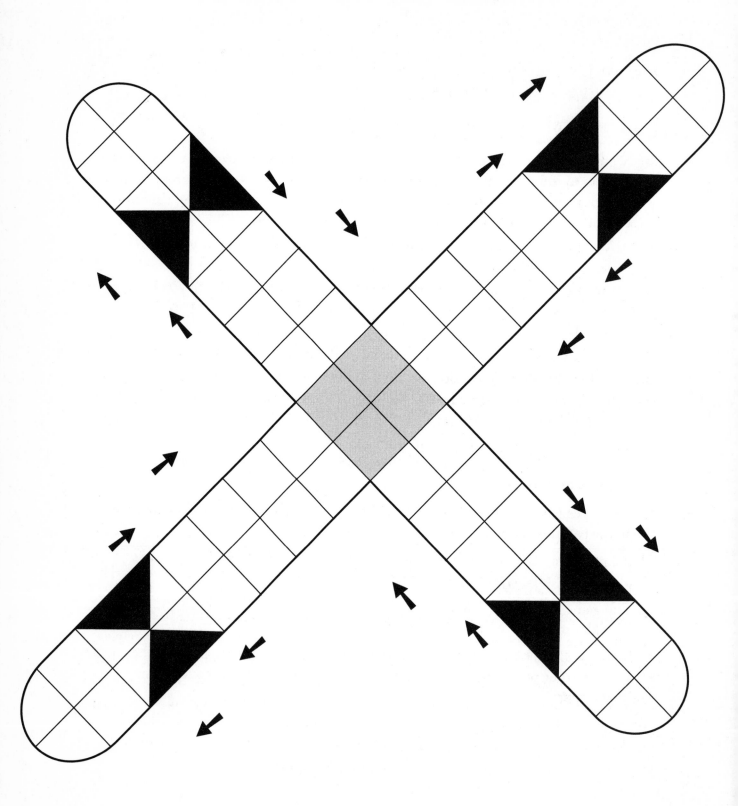

Mayas, Aztecs, Incas Scholastic Teaching Resources

CONTRIBUTIONS AND QUESTIONS

Architecture

The architecture of the Aztecs was impressive. Their sacrificial temples, where about 20,000 people a year were sacrificed to their deities, were important and were in constant competition with other Aztec city temples. Instead of destroying the old temples, the Aztecs built on top of them. These temples resembled Egyptian pyramids except for the top, which was flattened and had two sections for sacrifices. Royal palaces for the emperor were extravagantly large and imposing structures. The palace was a two-story building with a large courtyard in the center. It was adorned with gold panels and elaborate paintings. Columns on the first floor supported the two-story building. The columns on the second floor supported the roof overhead. The palace was divided into four main rooms: reception chamber, emperor's personal apartment, large meeting room, and a tribute room. Here, the emperor greeted guests, lived his life, received news from messengers, and stored his gifts.

Medicine

The Aztecs used effective pharmaceutical means to help many of the ill in their society. After the Spanish invasion, doctors from Spain learned about herbal medicine from the Aztecs. They believed sickness was caused by supernatural means from their deities, magical means, or natural means. Each type of illness demanded a certain type of cure.

Montezuma II's Death

Montezuma II's death has been debated for centuries. After arriving in Tenochtitlán, Cortés placed Montezuma II under house arrest. He used the emperor as a puppet to control the Aztecs and was careful to not to anger the nobles. During this time, Spanish forces arrived on the coast from Cuba to arrest Cortés, who left Tenochtitlán to fight them. The Spaniard that Cortés left in charge of the city incited a revolt by attacking unarmed Aztecs during a sacred ceremony for the sun god Huitzilopochtli. When Cortés returned to the city, he brought Montezuma II out to calm the angry Aztecs. The Spaniards reported that Montezuma II's own people stoned him and that he died later of injuries. However, a Spanish chronicler wrote down an Aztec account of the incident, which reported that Montezuma II was found with five wounds inflicted by a Spanish dagger. Enraged by Montezuma II's death, the Aztecs killed hundreds of Spanish soldiers and forced Cortés out of the city. Eventually Cortés's forces defeated the Aztecs and took control of the empire.

ARCHITECTURAL PALACE BUILDERS, INC.

Students create a blueprint for an Aztec palace.

Materials

Internet access, paper, pencils

Here's How

① Share with students the background information about Aztec architecture on page 55. Tell students that they are members of an Aztec architectural firm that has been chosen to build a palace for the new emperor. To learn more about Aztec architecture, have students look at such Web sites as **http://library.thinkquest.org/10098/aztec.htm#Emperor's**.

② Divide students into small groups and have them choose a name for their architectural firm.

③ Tell students that their group must submit a blueprint for the emperor's approval. Their blueprint must include the following:
- ▲ two floors
- ▲ a large courtyard
- ▲ marble steps
- ▲ a reception chamber where the emperor can meet visitors
- ▲ a personal room for the emperor
- ▲ a main meeting chamber with a platform and chair for the emperor
- ▲ the emperor's tribute room, where gifts to the emperor can be stored
- ▲ walls with exquisite gold panels, paintings, and carvings

④ Depending on students' visual and spatial skills, offer students one or a choice of the following activities to create a blueprint:
- ▲ Cut out pictures showing colors, textures, and furnishing items from home and decorator magazines to show what each palace room might look like. Using one piece of construction paper per room, paste each cut-out item onto the appropriate room page, and label the pictures.
- ▲ Draw a floor plan using graph paper. (Students can use the floor plans in a visual reference book like David McCaulay's *Castle* as a model.)
- ▲ Draw a cross-section of part of the palace to give a more complete view of several rooms. (Again, provide students with architectural books and home and decorator magazines for models and ideas.)

⑤ Ask groups to present their blueprints to the class.

AN AZTEC MEDICAL PRESCRIPTION

Acting as Aztec physicians, students diagnose an illness and write a prescription for an ill Aztec.

Materials

paper, pens

Here's How

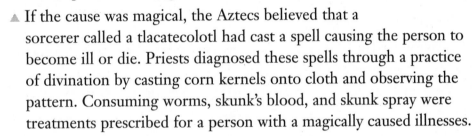

1. Share with students the background information about Aztec medicine on page 55. Then share the following information about how to treat illnesses with Aztec medicine:

   ▲ If the cause of sickness was supernatural, the person had to present offerings and confess to a priest.

   ▲ If the cause was magical, the Aztecs believed that a sorcerer called a tlacatecolotl had cast a spell causing the person to become ill or die. Priests diagnosed these spells through a practice of divination by casting corn kernels onto cloth and observing the pattern. Consuming worms, skunk's blood, and skunk spray were treatments prescribed for a person with a magically caused illnesses.

   ▲ Male and female physicians treated naturally caused illnesses by using herbs, cleaning wounds, using bandages, sucking out the venom of snake bites, setting broken bones with plaster casts and splints, and other remedies.

2. Tell students that they will be writing a prescription on a sheet of paper for an Aztec who is ill.

3. Have students write the name of the patient, the type of illness (supernatural, magical, or natural), and an Aztec remedy to treat the illness.

Extension

Have students create a help-wanted classified advertisement for Aztec physicians.

THE MYSTERY OF MONTEZUMA II'S DEATH

Students participate in a courtroom simulation to investigate Montezuma II's death.

Materials

A Court Case (page 59), index cards, pens, reference books, Internet access

1. Distribute *A Court Case* to students and ask them to read it. Tell students that the controversy surrounding Montezuma II's death will be solved in court by one judge. Appoint one person to act as a judge.

2. Divide the remaining students into two opposing legal teams. Appoint one team to represent the Aztecs and one team to represent the Spanish. Ask students to create names for their teams, or legal firms.

3. Have teams prepare their arguments for the judge. Allow students to conduct further research for their cases about Montezuma II's death using reference books and Web sites such as **www.pbs.org/conquistadors/cortes/cortes_a00.html**. Encourage teams to write their arguments on index cards.

4. Ask the student playing the judge to research possible Aztec awards and punishments for the case.

5. Have teams present their arguments before the judge. Teams may wish to select one member to present their cases. Allow the judge to rule as he or she sees fit. Instruct the judge to hand down a punishment for the loser and an award for the winner.

A COURT CASE

Most history books and records today explain that the Aztec emperor Montezuma II's own people stoned him to death. However, a Spanish chronicler named Friar Diego Duran wrote an Aztec account of the event, which claimed that Montezuma II was found with five wounds from a Spanish dagger. Who's telling the truth about Montezuma II's death?

Your team will prepare a legal argument as to who is responsible for the death of Montezuma II. The argument will be presented before an unbiased judge, who will make a final decision on the matter. The judge will grant an award to the winner and a penalty to the loser.

The facts leading up to the death of Montezuma II are as follows:

✓ Hernán Cortés and his forces had taken over the city of Tenochtitlán and placed Montezuma II under house arrest. Cortés was using the emperor as a puppet to control the Aztecs.

✓ Spanish forces from Cuba arrived to arrest Cortés, who had refused to obey orders from his superior. Cortés left Tenochtitlán for the coast to fight these forces.

✓ While he was away, Cortés left another Spanish officer in charge of Tenochtitlán. This officer imprisoned and killed several Aztec leaders. He also ordered the slaughter of Aztecs during their festival of the sun god, Huitzilopochtli.

✓ Cortés returned to a city in chaos, with the Aztecs in revolt.

✓ Cortés forced Montezuma II to speak to the Aztecs in an attempt to calm the crowd.

✓ When Montezuma II tried to speak to his people, the Aztecs stoned their own ruler out of anger, the Spanish claimed. They said he later died of injuries from the stoning.

✓ An Aztec account says that Montezuma II was found with five wounds from a Spanish dagger.

✓ After Montezuma II's death, the Aztecs became enraged and chased the Spaniards out of Tenochtitlán.

✓ The Spanish later returned and conquered the city.

THE INCAS

Map and Time Line

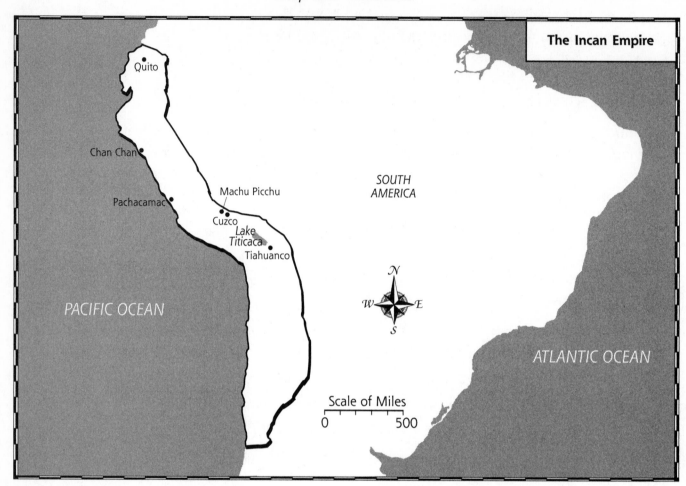

The Incan Empire

Quito

Chan Chan

Machu Picchu

Pachacamac

Cuzco

Lake Titicaca

Tiahuanco

SOUTH AMERICA

PACIFIC OCEAN

ATLANTIC OCEAN

N
W · E
S

Scale of Miles
0 ____ 500

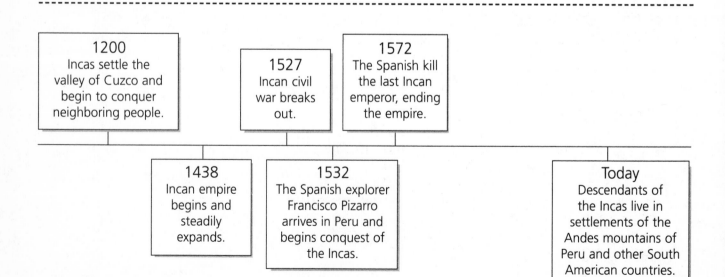

1200
Incas settle the valley of Cuzco and begin to conquer neighboring people.

1527
Incan civil war breaks out.

1572
The Spanish kill the last Incan emperor, ending the empire.

1438
Incan empire begins and steadily expands.

1532
The Spanish explorer Francisco Pizarro arrives in Peru and begins conquest of the Incas.

Today
Descendants of the Incas live in settlements of the Andes mountains of Peru and other South American countries.

GOVERNMENT, RULERS, AND CONQUESTS

Quipu

The Incan government did not have a formal writing system but kept track of important records using colored cords and knots called a quipu. The colors of the string represented different goods or resources. For example, yellow might be used for gold and red for an army. Much about how the quipu was used still remains a mystery, but an archaeologist named Leland Locke deciphered some of the puzzle in the 1920s. It is believed that the location of the knots on the strings could be interpreted as representing a base 10 system. For example, moving from the top of the string to the bottom would be the ten thousands place, thousands place, hundreds place, tens place, and units/ones place. The emperor appointed several keepers of the knot to each town. Large towns had as many as 30 keepers of the knot. Couriers could carry the quipu to relay information from town to town. Couriers also provided an oral message to accompany the quipu, since it was so complex. The quipu was then read by trained readers.

Government

The Sapa Inca, or emperor, was considered to be the sun god, Inti. The emperor often named his own successor. Rulers under the Sapa Inca were related, and the emperor would marry his sister to keep the bloodline pure. The Sapa Inca kept a tight reign on his people and land. There were 1,111 rulers for every 10,000 people. Four governors each ruled a quarter of the empire. Under each governor, ten district governors supervised 10,000 people. Under the district governors, a village leader managed 1,000 people. Ten village foremen served under a village leader and kept track of 100 people. Last of all, village officials oversaw ten people. The rule of the Sapa Inca was absolute, except when an uprising occurred, often resulting from an uncertain successor. One such incident occurred in the early 1500s with the death of the emperor Huayna Capac, who may have had smallpox. Huayna Capac chose one of his sons to succeed him, but his son died shortly before he did. Upon the emperor's death, the empire was divided between two of his sons—with the northern part, including Quito, under Atahualpa and the southern part, including the capital of Cuzco, under Huascar. The two brothers fought in a civil war, which weakened the empire as the Spanish arrived in the early 1500s.

The Spanish Conquest

Led by Francisco Pizarro in 1532, the Spanish invaders were driven by a desire for gold and glory. Pizarro led about 160 men to victory over the Incas, defeating Atahualpa's army. Even though a ransom was paid for Atahualpa's life, the Spanish executed him and kept the gold. The Incas continued to fight against the Spanish for decades. In 1572 the Spanish killed the last Incan emperor, Tupac Amarú, and the Incan empire was defeated.

HELP WANTED: INCAN RECORD KEEPERS

Students create and explain their own quipu.

Materials

Using Quipu Math (page 63), thin string, bowls of water, food coloring, paper towels or old newspaper

Here's How

❶ Share with students the background information about the quipu on page 61.

❷ Distribute copies of *Using Quipu Math* to students. Help students to read the quipu in the first diagram. Then have students identify the quipu numbers in the second diagram.

❸ As students work on *Using Quipu Math*, prepare bowls with different food colorings for dyeing the quipu. Place them in a location that students can access.

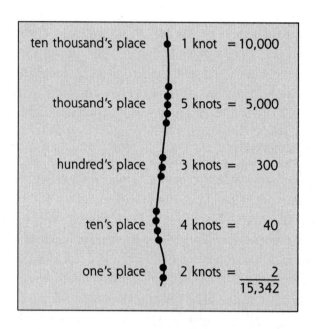

ten thousand's place	1 knot	= 10,000
thousand's place	5 knots	= 5,000
hundred's place	3 knots	= 300
ten's place	4 knots	= 40
one's place	2 knots	= 2
		15,342

❹ Tell students that the Sapa Inca is looking to appoint a new record keeper to your village. The record keeper must be someone who can count accurately, can tie knots, and can count in a base 10 system. This accountant will need to keep the records of food within the village so that the Sapa Inca will know if there is any threat of famine. The storehouse contains potatoes, corn, lima beans, peppers, tomatoes, squash, berries, and nuts.

❺ Tell students that they will have a chance to impress the emperor by submitting a sample quipu for inspection. Record keepers will be asked to explain their quipu to the Sapa Inca.

❻ Have students cut pieces of string and soak them in bowls of food coloring. After letting the strings dry on old newspaper or paper towels, students assemble their quipu.

❼ Allow students to present their quipu to the class.

Answers:

1. 23 2. 471 3. 1,954 4. 2,328 5. 10,634

USING QUIPU MATH

It is believed that the Incas used a base 10 system, which is shown on knotted strings called quipu. The location of each knot on the string indicated its place value. For example, the knots, moving from the top of the string to the bottom, would represent the ten thousands place, thousands place, hundreds place, tens place, and ones place.

Look at the quipu below. Identify the numbers shown on each of the five strings.

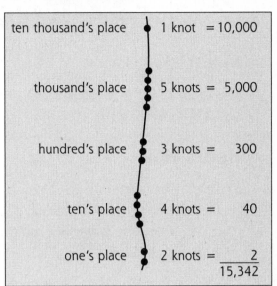

ten thousand's place	1 knot	= 10,000
thousand's place	5 knots	= 5,000
hundred's place	3 knots	= 300
ten's place	4 knots	= 40
one's place	2 knots	= 2
		15,342

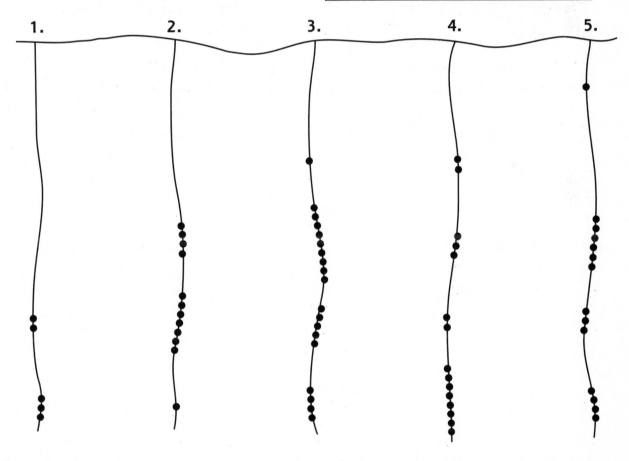

1. _____

2. _____

3. _____

4. _____

5. _____

A CIVIL WAR SIMULATION

Students create a computer simulation about the Incan civil war between Huascar and Atahualpa.

Materials

Sim Inca: A New Computer Game (page 65), pencils or pens, paper, posterboard, markers

Here's How

① Divide students into small groups. Distribute copies of *Sim Inca: A New Computer Game* to each group, and read the directions aloud.

② Ask students to share about computer games that they have played. Ask them to analyze how these games work.

③ Have groups brainstorm ideas for their computer games. Remind groups that they should incorporate the information under "The War of Two Brothers" on *Sim Inca: A New Computer Game* into their computer games. Direct groups to include possible actions and consequences of each action. Point out that this includes the actions of the two Incan leaders—Huascar and Atahualpa—and their generals. Ask groups to write down their ideas on a piece of paper.

④ Have groups use markers and posterboard to create a diagram in the form of a web that shows how to play their computer games. Explain that the web should show the moves that a player can make— and the consequences of those moves.

⑤ Allow groups to present their games to the class. Instruct the class to play the part of company members.

SIM INCA: A NEW COMPUTER GAME

You have been selected by a top computer company to create a computer game that simulates an Incan civil war. Use the information below to design your game. Then present your design in a company meeting. Your presentation must look professional and be easy to follow.

The War of Two Brothers

◎ Upon the death of the Sapa Inca Huayna Capac, the Incan empire became split between two of the emperor's sons— Atahualpa and Huascar. In the northern part of the empire, including Quito, was the fierce warrior Atahualpa. Huascar, the rightful heir to the throne, ruled the southern half of the empire, with the capital of Cuzco.

◎ Huascar summoned his brother, Atahualpa, to Cuzco for their father's funeral and to see himself coronated as emperor.

◎ Atahualpa feared for his life and did not go to Cuzco. Instead he sent gifts with ambassadors who reassured Huascar of Atahualpa's loyalty to him.

◎ Angry with his brother, Huascar burned the gifts and killed the ambassadors. He also sent an army to Quito led by his general Huanca Auqui.

◎ Atahualpa mobilized his generals, Chalcuchima and Quizquiz, to meet general Huanca Auqui in Tumibamba.

◎ In Tumibamba Atahualpa's army defeated Huascar's army in two days. Huascar's army was no match for the war experience of Atahualpa.

◎ Atahualpa began a full-scale invasion of Peru, making Cuzco his final destination. Although Huascar's army was the largest in Incan history, it fled before Atahualpa's skilled fighters.

◎ Huascar's army waited for Atahualpa's forces at the Cotapampa River outside of Cuzco.

◎ Huascar pled with the gods for help. As Atahualpa's forces walked through the tall grass, Huascar had the grass set on fire to destroy Atahualpa's army.

◎ Huascar called back his men to celebrate their victory.

◎ In the night, Chalcuchima and Quizquiz rallied Atahualpa's army to set a trap for Huascar near a ravine.

◎ The next morning, Huascar's army walked into the trap, and their general was captured.

◎ Huascar's general was tortured into revealing that Huascar and some soldiers would come down the ravine shortly.

◎ Huascar's army was defeated, and general Chalcuchima captured Huascar off of his litter.

◎ Chalcuchima climbed aboard the litter and had it taken to Huascar's base camp.

◎ Huascar's army fled when they saw that Huascar was not riding on the litter.

◎ Chalcuchima led Atahualpa's army into Cuzco, where Atahualpa claimed the throne.

THE CONQUEST OF PIZARRO

Students launch a political campaign to gain Incan soldiers for their army.

Materials

posterboard, markers, pens

Here's How

1. Divide students into two different groups. One group will be followers of Manco Capac II and the other group will be Spanish explorers.

2. Give the following background information to groups:

> After the civil war, the Spanish explorer Francisco Pizarro and about 200 men took control of the empire. They killed Atahualpa and set up a ruler to act as a puppet. His name was Manco Capac II—another son of the Sapa Inca Huayna Capac. Manco asked Pizarro's brother, Hernando, to release him so that he could go pray to a shrine. Hernando believed him and let him go. Manco used this new freedom to call on Incas to revolt against the Spanish. In 1536, as the Spanish were quarreling among themselves, Manco led 100,000 in a revolt against the Spanish in Cuzco. His army surrounded Cuzco and held it under siege for a year. Some Incas betrayed Manco and smuggled food and supplies to the Spanish. When the Spanish reinforcements arrived, about 20,000 of Manco's men retreated into the Andes north of Cuzco and carried out guerrilla-warfare attacks on the Spanish. These men set up a new village called Vilcabamba. The rule of the Incas lasted for three and a half decades with three of Manco's sons succeeding him as the Sapa Inca. The Spanish finally caught the last ruling Inca, named Tupac Amarú. He was given a trial and beheaded. The Incan rulers were no more.

3. Have students work in pairs to complete a T-chart for their group: "Spanish Rule: Pros/Cons" or "Incan Rule: Pros/Cons." For example, students might include "protection from enemies" under Pros for Spanish rule and "gold will be seized and taken away" under Cons. Share the ideas as a class so that each group hears the benefits and drawbacks of leadership from both sides.

4. Tell the Incan and Spanish groups that they will each launch a campaign to get Incas on their side. Explain that they can use modern advertising techniques such as television commercials, Internet Web sites, billboards, and other devices. Ask groups to agree on an idea and create a sample of their idea on posterboard.

5. Have students present their campaign ideas to the class.

DAILY LIFE

Origins of the Incas

There are many different legends about the origins of the Incas, although all name Manco Capac as the founder of the empire. In one version the sun god Inti instructs Manco Capac and his sister-wife, Mama Ocllo, to find the best land for the Incas using a golden rod. The Incan emperor was believed to be a direct descendant of the sun god, and the Incas called themselves "the Children of the Sun." Archaeological evidence supports the theory that the first Americans came from Asia tens of thousands of years ago in search of game to hunt. Recent evidence shows that people may have lived as long as 33,000 years ago in what is now Chile. In about 1200 the Incas began to rule their neighbors, and by 1438 the empire was established. The Incas made alliances with other groups of people and grew in numbers by conquering them. In the 1400s the Incas expanded their territory to include areas of what are now Argentina, Bolivia, Chile, Colombia, Ecuador, and Peru.

Incan Textiles

Incan textiles have survived many centuries and are still popular in South America today. Women wove llama wool and cotton into cloth and collected dyes from plants to make the cloth colorful. They wove intricate and colorful designs ranging from simple stripes to complex patterns. In the highlands, the Incas wore mostly wool clothing, while those along the coast wore mostly cotton. Women wore dresses tied at the waist with a sash. They also wore shawls, with a jewelry pin at the shoulder, and necklaces. Men wore tunics or breechcloths, as well as ponchos. Some Incas decorated their clothing with feathers from tropical birds. Men wore elaborate round earplugs that were up to two inches in diameter and made of shells, gold, or silver. Men might also wear bracelets, necklaces, and headdresses and carry a small bag filled with personal items. The clothes of the nobility were made from finer cloth.

Mummy Bundles

The Incas carefully preserved their dead by mummification and wrapped them in bundles with many layers of cloth. These bundles might include up to seven people, weigh up to 500 pounds, and stand six feet tall. Because the Incas believed that the souls of the dead kept in touch with those still living, certain possessions of the deceased were wrapped within each layer, including valuable personal possessions, everyday items, and food for use in the underworld. Archaeologists have found some ancient Incan mummies in almost perfect condition because of the dry, cold climate of the Andes. The layering is so extensive that it can take archaeologists at least two months to open one mummy bundle. The Incas treated royal mummies as if they were still living and even consulted them for advice.

A ONE-ACT PLAY

Students collaborate to produce a play about an Incan creation myth.

Materials

Children of the Sun (pages 69–71); items such as pots, pans, and whistles to create sounds; items such as paper, markers, tape, and a pole, to create props and masks

Here's How

❶ Distribute copies of *Children of the Sun* to students. Share with students the background information on page 67 about the origins of the Incas. Emphasize that this play presents one version of the Incas' origins.

❷ Tell students that putting on a play is a collaborative effort that includes a director, performers, and artists who create sound, lighting, props, and costumes. Explain that a director oversees the entire production. Point out that a director helps performers with their lines and movements. Explain that the sound, prop, and costume artists discuss their ideas with the director.

❸ You may wish to have students put their names in a hat to assign jobs or assign them yourself. You will need one director, eight performers, and groups to work on sound, props, and costumes.

❹ Ask the sound, props, and costume groups to come up with a plan for the play and discuss it with the director. For example, the sound artists should decide where they want to create special sounds in the play, the prop artists should decide what props they want to create or use, and the costume artists might want to create masks for the performers.

❺ Allow the sound, prop, and costume groups to work on their items. Have the director and performers rehearse the play.

❻ You may wish to present a final performance to another class.

CHILDREN OF THE SUN

A legend of the origins of the first Incan rulers.

> **Cast in order of appearance:**
> Narrator
> Inti (the father sun god)
> Manco Capac (Inti's son and husband to his
>   sister, Mama Ocllo)
> Mama Ocllo (Inti's daughter and wife to her
>   brother, Manco Capac)
> Four People

Narrator: Inti, the sun god, was deep in thought as he looked down on Earth one day. His children, Manco Capac and Mama Ocllo, were in his presence.

Inti: These poor people. They act just like wild beasts. Don't you think so, Manco Capac?

Manco Capac: Not only do I agree with you, but I would go a step further. . . . They are pathetic! They don't even have homes except for the shelter from the rock ledges hanging on the sides of the mountains.

Mama Ocllo: (*laughing*) Yes, and did you ever miss a sight yesterday! I saw several people eating raw meat!

(*They all groan.*)

Inti: These people need help!

(*All agree nodding their heads.*)

I've been thinking about this for some time. I want both of you to go down to the people and help them.

Manco Capac: Sure, we'll help in any way you need us to.

Mama Ocllo: It would be an honor to go! Where will you send us? What should I pack for the journey?

CHILDREN OF THE SUN (Continued)

Inti: I've decided to send you to the Rock of the Cat. It's an island in the middle of a lake in the Andes mountains right between Peru and Bolivia. See here on the map?

(Inti shows a map to Mama and Manco.)

Mama Ocllo: Oh, that's in Lake Titicaca! I just love its blue icy waters that reflect the clear sky!

Manco Capac: Yes, it's the largest of the 41 islands in the lake. It is also called Titicaca Island.

Inti: Before you leave, I have a special gift for you. Take this rod of gold. You can decide what direction to go once you are at Titicaca Island. Once you stop to rest, place this rod of gold as far into the ground as you can. If it only sinks in a few inches, then that is not the right place for you. You will know when you get to the right place because the earth will swallow the rod.

Manco Capac: Is that where we will build a city for the people, where they can worship you?

Inti: Yes. You will be king of all the people who accept me. You must always remember to rule with justice and mercy and follow my example. Love the people as I have loved you, my children.

Narrator: Manco Capac and Mama Ocllo floated down to Titicaca Island and emerged from the waters.

Mama Ocllo: Let's go north! I'm sure the city will be to the north of where we are!

Narrator: They walked for a while and then Manco Capac used the golden rod. He pushed with all his strength, but the rod would only go down about an inch.

Manco Capac: We've been walking for many days. Let's try the rod again. Here is a beautiful area called the Valley of Cuzco. Maybe this is the right location for the city!

Mama Ocllo: I love how snowcapped mountains surround it. Yes, try the rod again.

Narrator: Before Manco could even try to push the rod into the earth, the fertile ground swallowed it right up.

(Both Manco Capac and Mama Ocllo jump and shout for joy.)

Manco Capac: Now the hard part of our journey begins. We have to go our separate ways and tell people about our mission.

XOX

CHILDREN OF THE SUN *(Continued)*

Mama Ocllo: I'll go to the south and you go to the north.

(*They part ways.*)

Narrator: Mama Ocllo came upon some people hunting for food in a field.

Mama Ocllo: Hello! I'm a Child of the Sun, and I've come down from the sky to help you. Come follow me, and you will be happy.

Person 1:   If I do follow you, will you show me how to weave beautiful clothing like yours?

Person 2:   Yes, I love how it sparkles in the sun!

Mama Ocllo: I'll teach you much more than just weaving. You will learn how to spin the thread and cook wonderful meals for your family. But most important, I'll teach you how to worship the sun god.

Narrator: They all wandered off together to see where their city would be built. Meanwhile, Manco Capac met some people as he traveled north.

Manco Capac: Hello! I am a Child of the Sun, and I've come down from the sky to help you! Come with me and I'll teach you how to build your own house so that your family will have a permanent shelter.

Person 3:   I'm hungry. Can you teach me how to find food?

Manco Capac: I'll do better than that. I'll teach you how to find seeds for planting and how to farm the land. You will also learn about my father, the sun god.

Person 4:   I've been wanting something like this! Let me go back and tell my relatives, and we will all follow you there.

Narrator: Everyone the Children of the Sun encountered wanted to go with them. These people learned to select seeds, make plows, till the soil, and irrigate the fields. They became skilled at weaving cloth from wool and cotton. And most important, they learned to worship the sun god.

The End

EXCLUSIVELY INCA:
A NEW CLOTHING CATALOG COMPANY

Students create a catalog for Incan attire.

Materials

copies of clothing catalogs and
advertisements, paper, pencils, pens,
colored pencils or markers

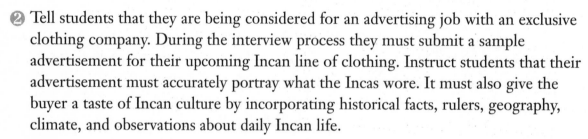

Here's How

1. Have students read advertisements
   from various clothing catalogs
   such as the J. Peterman Company's
   catalog or Web site. Ask students
   to locate advertisements that are written with a creative flair and incorporate a story
   about the clothing. They will use these ads as a model for writing their own.

2. Tell students that they are being considered for an advertising job with an exclusive
   clothing company. During the interview process they must submit a sample
   advertisement for their upcoming Incan line of clothing. Instruct students that their
   advertisement must accurately portray what the Incas wore. It must also give the
   buyer a taste of Incan culture by incorporating historical facts, rulers, geography,
   climate, and observations about daily Incan life.

3. Share with students the background information about Incan textiles on page 67.
   Have students view references relating to Incan textiles. These might include
   books such as César Paternosto's *The Stone and the Thread: Andean Roots of Abstract
   Art* (University of Texas Press, 1996) or Web sites such as Descendants of the Incas:
   Chinchero Patterns at **http://www.incas.org/patterns_srce.html** or Peru Image
   Collection at **http://exchanges.state.gov/culprop/peru/textile/sect2.htm**.

4. Have students write their descriptions and create a sketch for their advertisements.

5. Bind these advertisements together to make an Incan catalog and distribute it to students.

Extension

Ask students how Incan clothing could have been improved, knowing what we know
today about the warmth and durability of various fabrics. Have students recommend
a modernized piece of Incan clothing and provide logical reasons for their answer.

WRAPPING INCAN MUMMIES

Students create their own mummy bundles.

Materials

pencils, paper, string, scissors, magazines and catalogs

Here's How

1. Share with students the background information about Incan mummy bundles on page 67. Have students view Web sites such as **http://www.nationalgeographic .com/channel/inca/** for information about how the Inca bundled their deceased.

2. Explain that the items bundled with a mummy give clues about that person. For example, a mace might mean that the person had been a warrior, and a pair of sandals, feathers, or a headdress might indicate that the person had high status in society. Tell students about other items found in the Incan mummy bundles, such as gourds, which were used as bowls or containers; yarn combs, which were used in textile making; and sacred shells.

3. Tell students that they will wrap their own mummies. Ask them to think about what items to include in their mummy bundles, and what these items will reveal about their mummies.

4. Explain to students that Incan adults were often buried in a fetal position. Have students draw the outline of a person in a fetal position and cut it out. Direct students to wrap this figure in paper and string.

5. Ask students to search though magazines and catalogs to find items to bury with their mummies. Have them cut out their selected items.

6. Have students set each item in a separate layer, wrapping paper and string around the object and the previous layer.

7. After students have wrapped their bundles with several layers, have them trade bundles with a partner. Allow partners to unwrap and decipher each other's mummy bundles. Have the student who unwrapped the bundle speculate about the status and occupation of the mummy and have the partner confirm the idea or explain a different reason for including the items.

CONTRIBUTIONS AND QUESTIONS

Machu Picchu

In 1911 a historian named Hiram Bingham rediscovered Machu Picchu, hidden in the clouds about 8,000 feet above sea level. This five-square-mile city was at first believed to have been a ceremonial sacred city and a training place for priestesses and noble women. Today many scholars believe that the city may have been a royal or religious retreat center. Machu Picchu included agricultural terraces and fresh water from springs. It contained bathhouses, palaces, temples, storage rooms, an astronomical structure, and about 150 houses—most made from granite blocks cut with bronze or stone tools. These blocks were smoothed down with sand. The joints of the stones fit together so perfectly that the blade of a knife could not penetrate between stones. Up to ten homes might be grouped together through connections of narrow alleys and aligned on narrow terraces or around a central courtyard. These houses rarely had windows. Some were two stories tall. Rope ladders were probably used to reach the second story. The thatched roofs were steep, and the doorways were shaped like trapezoids.

Astronomy

The Incas were avid astronomers. Not only did they worship the sun, but they also used the sun to help them make plans for planting and harvesting crops. To do this, they created *intihuatanas*, or sundials. Intihuatana means "hitching post of the sun." The sundial's shadow disappeared during the spring and fall equinoxes—the times for planting and harvesting. Some scholars believe that large celebrations and festivals were held during the summer and winter solstices. The Incas may have symbolically tied the sun to the intihuatana to keep it from straying away. It was thought that touching the intihuatana was a spiritual experience for the Incas. As the Spanish made their way through the Incan empire, they broke each intihuatana because of its relationship with worshiping the sun god. Because the Spanish never found the elusive village of Machu Picchu, only the intihuatana at Machu Picchu remains intact.

Incan Bridges

The Incan communities were built on some of the Andes mountains. To make travel easier over the deep river gorges below, the Incas erected suspension bridges from mountain to mountain. Twisted ropes of plants—such as grass or vines—held these bridges that lasted for hundreds of years. These cables were as thick as a person's leg and were twisted in such a way to make the bridge strong enough to walk upon. The cables were replaced about every two years to make sure they remained in good condition, and the bridges were periodically repaired. Some of the bridges extended 330 feet in length. Some scholars believe that if the Incas would have been willing to cut the bridges, the Spaniards could have been defeated. These suspension bridges allowed the Spanish to cross dangerous rivers and go from village to village.

REAL-ESTATE ADS AT MACHU PICCHU

Students write a real-estate advertisement for a house for sale at Machu Picchu.

Materials

Real-estate advertisements from local newspapers, paper, pens, pencils, colored pencils or markers

Here's How

❶ Share with students the background information about the homes at Machu Picchu on page 74. Have students view pictures from books such as Elizabeth Gemming's *Lost City in the Clouds: The Discovery of Machu Picchu* (Penguin, 1980). Students can also find information on such Web sites as these:

http://emuseum.mnsu.edu/prehistory/latinamerica /south/sites/machu_picchu.html

http://www.sacredsites.com/2nd56/21422.html

http://www.raingod.com/angus/Gallery/Photos /SouthAmerica/Peru/IncaTrail.html

http://www.millville.org/Workshops_f/Acker_Inca/eg_inca_9.htm

❷ Tell students that they will write a real-estate advertisement for a house for sale at Machu Picchu.

❸ Have students look at real-estate ads in newspapers to get an idea of how to write their advertisements.

❹ Have students write their advertisements. Then have them draw pictures of their homes to go along with their advertisements.

❺ Allow students to share their advertisements with the class.

INCAN ASTRONOMERS: TRACKING THE SUN

Students learn about the astronomy of the Incas and study the movements of the sun.

Materials

paper plates, clay, popsicle sticks, weights (such as stones), pens

Here's How

❶ Share with students the background information about the Incas and astronomy on page 74. Emphasize that the Incas used the movements of the sun to help them plant and harvest their crops. Ask students if anyone knows how a sundial works. Allow time for responses.

❷ Tell students that they will track the movement of the sun. Have students place a thumb-size amount of clay in the middle of a paper plate.

❸ Instruct students to stand a popsicle stick in the center of the plate by anchoring it in the clay.

❹ Have students place their plates outside. You may need to weigh down the plates with stones to keep them from blowing away. The paper plate should not be moved during this entire experiment.

❺ Let students go outside to periodically track the movements of the sun on their paper plates. The point where the shadow falls should be marked along with the time of day. Allow students to place at least four recordings on their plate.

❻ At the end of the allotted time, have students observe and comment on their records.

Extension

Have students plan a sun festival for the winter and summer solstices at Machu Picchu. Encourage students to select the food and festival events such as entertainment, ritual dances, and guest speakers.

INCAN SUSPENSION BRIDGES

Students make a model of an Incan suspension bridge.

Materials

books about the world's bridges; Internet access; paper; pencils; per group: *Designing a Bridge* (page 78), ten sheets of paper, 10 cm of masking tape, one coffee can filled with 500 ml (two cups) of water

Here's How

1. Have students research famous bridges around the world in reference books such as *Bridges: Amazing Structures to Design, Build & Test* by Carol A. Johnmann and Elizabeth J. Rieth and *Bridges* by Etta Kaner. Students may also view Incan bridges at **http://www.bu.edu/bridge/archive/2003/03-21/bridge.html** and at **http://www.civl.port.ac.uk/comp_prog/bridges1/index.htm**. Have students analyze the differences and similarities among the bridges that they have researched by comparing their style, building material, size, and shape.

2. Share with students the background information about Incan bridges on page 74. Have students compare other bridges with these ancient bridges.

3. Divide students into groups of three. Give each group a copy of *Designing a Bridge*. Tell groups that they are ancient Incan engineers and are bidding on a proposal to build a suspension bridge across a local river. Explain that groups must build a model of their bridge and prove that their bridge can support weight. Ask groups to enter a name for their engineering company on *Designing a Bridge*.

4. Tell groups that their goal is to build a strong suspension bridge that costs the least. Direct groups to construct an economical suspension bridge that is at least 18 inches in length that can support a coffee can filled with 500 ml of water. Tell groups that they will have the following materials available to them: ten sheets of notebook paper, 10 cm of masking tape, and a coffee can filled with 500 ml of water. Explain to groups that each sheet of notebook paper that they use will cost $10 and each centimeter of tape will cost $15. Explain that the masking tape will be used to secure the bridge between two desks—representing two mountains—from end to end. Tell groups that they will only be charged for the materials that they actually use on their bridges.

5. Ask groups to create designs for their bridges on a piece of paper. Then let them begin construction. (To increase the challenge, give students a time limit.) Have students calculate how much their bridges cost to build. Then have them record the cost and a sketch of their final design on *Designing a Bridge*.

6. Give awards for the most creative design, the longest, the strongest (add more weight to see what it can withstand), and the least expensive.

DESIGNING A BRIDGE

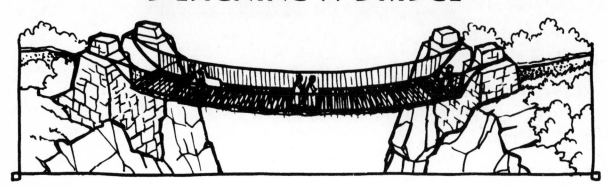

Name of your Incan engineering firm: _____

_____

Available Materials:

10 sheets of notebook paper at $10 a sheet

10 cm of masking tape at $15 a cm

1 coffee can with 500 ml (2 cups) of water

total

Cost for materials: (paper @ $10 x ___ = $ ___) + (tape @ $15 x ___ = $ ___) = $ _____

Sketch of your bridge:

BIBLIOGRAPHY

Books for Students

Baquedano, Elizabeth. *Eyewitness Aztec, Inca, & Maya*. DK Publishing, 2000.

Drew, David. *Inca Life*. Barron's Educational Series, 2000.

Fisher, Leonard Everett. *Gods and Goddesses of the Ancient Maya*. Holiday House, 1999.

Green, Jen, et al. *The Encyclopedia of the Ancient Americans*. Anness Publishing, 2001.

Hicks, Peter. *The Aztecs*. Raintree Publishers, 1998.

Johnmann, Carol A., and Elizabeth J. Rieth. *Bridges: Amazing Structures to Design, Build & Test*. Williamson, 1999.

Kaner, Etta. *Bridges*. Kids Can Press, 1995.

Lourie, Peter. *Lost Treasure of the Inca*. Boyds Mills Press, 1999.

Macdonald, Fiona. *How Would You Survive as an Aztec?* Sagebrush Education Resources, 1997.

————. *Inca Town*. Sagebrush Education Resources, 1999.

————. *Step Into the . . . Aztec & Mayan Worlds*. Anness Publishing, 1998.

McCaulay, David. *Castle*. Houghton Mifflin, 1983. (architectural drawings and floor plans)

Montejo, Victor. *The Bird Who Cleans the World and Other Mayan Fables*. Translated by Wallace Kaufman. Curbstone Press, 1991.

Meyer, Carolyn, and Charles Gallenkamp. *The Mystery of the Ancient Maya*. Rev. ed. Simon & Schuster Children's, 1995.

Reinhard, Johan. *Discovering the Inca Ice Maiden*. National Geographic Children's, 1998.

Steele, Philip. *The Aztec News*. Gareth Stevens Audio, 2000.

Stein, Richard Conrad. *The Aztec Empire*. Benchmark Books, 1995.

Wood, Tim. *The Aztecs*. Penguin Books, 1992.

————. *The Incas*. Viking, 1996.

BIBLIOGRAPHY (Continued)

Web Sites for Students

MAYAS

CyberSleuthKids Ancient Civilizations: Maya **http://cybersleuth-kids.com /sleuth/History/Ancient_Civilizations/Mayans/**

The Maya Astronomy Page **http://www.michielb.nl/maya**

Collapse: Why Do Civilizations Fall? (Looking for Clues at Copán) **http://www.learner.org/exhibits/collapse/copan/index.php**

Maya Links **http://www.jaguar-sun.com/links.html**

Rabbit in the Moon **http://www.halfmoon.org**

The Mesoamerican Ballgame **http://www.ballgame.org**

Nova Online: Lost King of the Maya **http://www.pbs.org/wgbh/nova/maya**

AZTECS

Aztec Architecture **http://library.thinkquest.org/10098/aztec.htm**

The Aztecs **http://home.freeuk.net/elloughton13/aztecs.htm**

CyberSleuthKids Ancient Civilizations: Aztec **http://cybersleuth-kids.com /sleuth/History/Ancient_Civilizations/Aztec/index.htm**

Sports and Games **http://emuseum.mnsu.edu/prehistory/latinamerica /topics/games.html**

INCAS

National Geographic News: Thousands of Inca Mummies Raised From Their Graves **http://news.nationalgeographic.com/news/2002/04/0410_020417_ incamummies.html**

National Geographic: Inca Rescue **http://magma.nationalgeographic.com/ngm/0205/feature5/index.html**

Machu Picchu, Peru **http://sacredsites.com/americas/peru/machu_picchu.html**